A Toolkit for the
Effective Teaching Assistant

The University of Plymouth's current Foundation Degree in Education (Teaching Assistants) stems from a decade of carefully developing and managing provision for support staff. As practising teachers all the contributors to this book have worked closely with teaching assistants and recognize the importance of their impact for pupils, teachers, schools and the curriculum. In 1995, the University commenced two new programmes, first, the Specialist Teacher Assistant Certificate (STAC) for TAs in mainstream schools and second, the Certificate of Higher Education for TAs in special schools. Both groups consisted of 20 TAs. In 1997 these programmes were united under the guidance of Richard Tyrer, the programme director. The numbers have risen dramatically in the subsequent period and currently there are over 1,000 TAs enrolled on the Foundation degree programme.

Richard Tyrer entered Higher Education after working in industry, like many of the TAs he works with. He believes such experience stood him in good stead in his chosen field of education, namely working with pupils with emotional, social and behavioural difficulties. The personal and professional achievements of so many TAs as a direct result of attendance at the programme that he has nurtured is a significant milestone in his career. He holds a BEd. from the University of Manchester, a BA from the University of London and an MA from the University of Exeter.

Chris Lee was a colleague in the early days of working with TAs in the 1990's and in fact taught the first ever session on the STAC programme. Chris has taught in both mainstream and special schools and is currently the Faculty of Education's programme director for the Masters degree programme. He recently successfully completed his doctorate and in 2004 Paul Chapman Publishing published his book *Preventing Bullying in Schools.*

Mary Pittman has taught and contributed to teacher training in Uganda, until 2001 she taught in a special school. She is a previous recipient of the national award of Special School Teacher of the Year. She is highly experienced in working alongside pupils with autistic tendencies and co-ordinates a charity for autistic young people. Prior to taking up her post at the University of Plymouth, she spent 6 months studying the TEACCH communication programme and Picture Exchange Communication System at Chapel Hill University in North Carolina. She has an MA from the University of Exeter.

Maureen Parker graduated from Keele University. She too has taught in special schools, but prior to her appointment to the University in 2000, she had established a very successful behavioural support programme at one of the country's largest secondary schools. She has just completed her MA with the University of Plymouth and has research interests in inclusive education and equality.

Stuart Gunn has a degree in psychology and in his early career worked in a unit for pupils with severe behavioural difficulties. Prior to his appointment he lectured in Further Education.

Mark Townsend initially trained as an architect before entering teaching. He taught in the same special school as Mary Pittman until 2001, when he was employed by the University. He organized a very successful ICT conference in Plymouth in 2003 and has recently researched and successfully published an article on the advantages of supporting the continuing professional development of TAs through distance learning.

A Toolkit for the Effective Teaching Assistant

Richard Tyrer, Stuart Gunn, Chris Lee,
Maureen Parker, Mary Pittman
and Mark Townsend

P·C·P
Paul Chapman
Publishing

© Richard Tyrer, Stuart Gunn, Chris Lee, Maureen Parker,
Mary Pittman and Mark Townsend 2004

First published 2004

Paul Chapman Publishing
A SAGE Publications Company
1 Oliver's Yard
55 City Road
London EC1Y 1SP

SAGE Publications Inc
2455 Teller Road
Thousand Oaks, California 91320

SAGE Publications India Pvt Ltd
B-42, Panchsheel Enclave
Post Box 4109
New Delhi 110 017

Library of Congress Control Number: 2004093825

A Catalogue record for this book is available from the British
Library

ISBN 1 4129 0060 3
ISBN 1 4129 0061 1 (pbk)

Production by Deer Park Productions, Tavistock, Devon
Typeset by TW Typesetting, Plymouth, Devon
Printed in Great Britain by Cromwell Press,
Trowbridge, Wiltshire

Contents

We have attempted to the best of our ability to give credit to every person whose work we have used or whose ideas we have incorporated in the text, and to honestly represent their views. If we have failed in any measure, then we apologize and resolve to make amends in future editions.

Introduction

In working alongside teaching assistants (TAs) on degree level programmes we have been privileged to be part of a rich, learning experience. An initiative that started life as a one term short course in 1995 has, without doubt, been driven forward by the enthusiasm, commitment and ability of TAs to combine work, study and a home life, to become the University of Plymouth's very successful Foundation degree in Education (Teaching Assistants).

In appreciation of what we have learned from TAs, we have produced, for a wider audience, a book that examines issues and challenges that appear to be fundamental in this demanding and difficult role.

Why a 'toolkit'?

Toolboxes contain a range of useful resources, often lovingly collected over time. Some will be used every day, others weekly and there will be those that have not been called into service for some while, but will, one day, prove essential for that 'special' task. In our opinion, a significant asset that TAs bring to education is their life experience. They are often able to offer schools high-level interpersonal skills that can add a different dimension in, and beyond, the classroom. It is most likely that these skills will have been accumulated and honed outside the formalized setting of the classroom. This book offers the notion of a 'toolkit' to allow TAs and colleagues to review and revise their thinking and practice about real issues and challenges in managing individuals, groups, colleagues and themselves in school.

In a rapidly changing educational environment the book focuses on combining the underpinning knowledge relevant to such issues and challenges with a basis for reflection. In this way it is hoped to enable TAs in all phases and types of schooling to examine their personal and professional philosophy and practice. I-35t will, hopefully, provide a steppingstone to the kind of critical and reflective study needed as a basis for those who wish to continue into higher education or to be considered for higher level teaching assistant (HLTA) status, or as most TAs tell us, 'just to be a better TA'.

The book contains practical examples of TAs at work, activities and references to other sources of further information about role and responsibilities. At the end of each chapter is a list of suggested reading allowing the reader to extend their interest and empower their dialogue through related texts that will contribute to the development of practice. In addition, it signals the relationship of the text to the higher level teaching assistants Standards produced by the Teacher Training Agency (TTA).

A Toolkit for the Effective Teaching Assistant explores specific themes with which TAs engage on a daily basis. Chapters on role and responsibilities, change, self esteem, team work and teaching and learning are supported by an introduction to ICT enabling TAs to assess their own values, attitudes and teaching skills in supporting pupils, teachers, the curriculum and their school.

Through relevant investigation, reflection and supportive dialogue with colleagues, it is envisaged that TAs will grow in confidence, knowledge, skill and understanding and enhance their role in a professionally orientated progression to boost all-round achievement.

It is important that any TA engaging with this book has the opportunity to discuss the contents with colleagues, to debate and develop their understanding of the subject matter and its implications for practice, and to make sure that any potential changes are in line with the agreed school policies and practice.

The reasons for this book

> Today, support staff are helping transform our schools' ability to raise standards of pupil achievement. Playing fulfilling roles in their own right, they are also freeing teachers to focus on teaching. But we now need to go even further. Over the coming years, we shall see a new stream of high level teaching assistants, pushing back the boundaries of what they can do in classrooms.
>
> (Morris, 2002, Foreword)

The recognition given to TAs is becoming increasingly important in the life of schools. A series of government initiatives has highlighted the value of their role in all phases and in all types of school provision.

The government continues to amend legislation such as changes in the Education (Teaching Work and Registration) England Regulations (DfES, 2002) and to allocate resources for the recruitment and training of TAs and support systems for their professional career development, including facilitating pathways to gain qualified teacher status (QTS). The important part that the government sees support staff playing in the Remodelling of the Workforce is reiterated in the *Handbook for Training Providers* for the award of HTLA:

> In 'Time for Standards', the government set out its plans for the reform of the school workforce. This included the recognition that support staff make an important contribution and that, with training and support, they could make a greater contribution to improving standards in schools
>
> (*HLTA Providers Handbook*, 2004, p. 4)

Initiatives, such as:

- the Induction programme for new TAs;

- National Occupational Standards (NOS) (www.lgemployers.gov.uk);

- Remodelling the Workforce (www.teachernet.gov.uk);

- Higher Level Teaching Assistant Standards (HLTA) (www.htla.gov.uk);

- routes Qualified Teacher Status (QTS) (www.canteach.gov.uk).

are changing the role and responsibilities of TAs.

Any aspiring professional must be prepared to evaluate their current set of attitudes, values and beliefs as well as assess how they might improve their practice in the work environment. However, it is still currently clear that there is little advance on issues such as pay and conditions of service.

How you might use this book

To use this book effectively it would be best to:

- be actively involved in an educational environment;

- have a desire to reflect on your knowledge, skill and understanding;

- be able to isolate and organize reading and study time;

- open an honest, two-way dialogue with teaching colleagues about issues in education today, but above all;

- examine your own thinking and practice in a 'constructively' critical manner.

To be most successful, you need colleagues with whom you can openly debate issues. You should also ensure there is someone in your school who knows that you are engaging with the issues in this book and with whom you can share your ideas and feelings – an in-school mentor, or 'critical friend'.

The Appendix contains all the higher level teaching assistant Standards for your consideration. If you are considering applying for HLTA status, then we suggest that you begin to identify and record evidence of your practice and begin to maintain a Professional Development Record (PDR) in which, over time, you can collect and record data and evidence about each HTLA Standard as guided by the TTA (www.hlta.gov.uk), or even our own HLTA website. (www.hltacommunitysouthwest.plymouth.ac.uk). It is not possible within this short book to consider all the Standards in depth and to your individual requirement. However, such Standards are likely to become an important 'measurement device' in your toolkit; therefore, we have inserted Standards where we believe they relate to the text. From these connections you might wish to explore your own practice and thinking more fully.

Activities are clearly indicated in boxes.

Standards are clearly indicated in shaded boxes.

All of the examples are based on what is perceived to be sound, effective practice. In line with ethical principles all the names have been changed to preserve the participants' anonymity. Suggestions for resources or areas of study are added at the end of each chapter.

This cannot be an exhaustive text; you will need to be able to access additional reading. However, if you are using this book as part of a degree-level qualification you will have appropriate resource support at your university and it will be expected that you will read more widely than just one prescribed textbook.

The structure of the book

This book is based directly on an holistic and fundamental approach to the role and personal development of the TA.

As this is a reference book, you need not read it page by page:

- ■ use the chapter headings or the index to find what you need;

- ■ read that section and then refer to any associated reading in the book, or recommended text;

- ■ do any associated activities and make any notes for your own future reference;

- ■ discuss the reading with colleagues;

- ■ record your findings and any evidence in your PDR.

Essentially, remember that you are a member of staff, recruited to play a specific and active role in school development. It is vital that your continuing professional development (CPD) is known to significant members of staff, fits in with school policy and culture, and that you play your part as a member of staff.

In Chapter 1, Richard Tyrer considers why the number of TAs has grown and the changes in philosophy that have supported this expansion. The bulk of the chapter, however, draws on a series of perceptions, both by and about TAs, on their role, responsibilities and place in school provision. This gives you an opportunity to begin to examine your own strengths and weaknesses.

In Chapter 2, Chris Lee considers the active role you play in school and suggests that you are increasingly involved as agents of change. You are invited to look at your attitude to change and to consider how changes can be planned and suported.

A school is a 'melting pot' of ideas and relationships. An effective relationship with colleagues is essential, and therefore Mary Pittman in Chapter 3 looks at the importance of being part of a team. She acknowledges the importance of teacher and TA partnerships in providing for pupil learning and suggests ways in which good collaborative practice can be, and has been, developed within schools.

In Chapter 4 Maureen Parker considers the impact of TAs in assessing and raising levels of self esteem. She considers how developing an understanding of self esteem and identifying specific strategies to support individual pupils can have an impact on learning. She has also identified aspects of self esteem that relate to the developing professional role of a TA.

The important contribution to raising academic standards by TAs should be underpinned by the development of equal level of skill, knowledge and understanding about teaching, learning and inter-personal relationships. In Chapter 5 Stuart Gunn provides a stimulus for reflecting on the complexity of pedagogy. He provides a brief theoretical background, before looking at some practical facets of learning and teaching.

Finally, the contribution of ICT to raising achievement and helping pupils, teachers, schools and TAs to improve their standards is considered in Chapter 6 by Mark Townsend. In this he provides an overview of some of the contemporary key developments which are affecting TAs, both in their roles as educators and as learners in this large and rapidly evolving subject area.

Questions you might ask yourself before you commence

- Have I identified an 'in-school' mentor or 'critical friend'?

- Have I identified ethical issues in discussing and writing about school life, for example, maintaining confidentiality?

- Where might I find further reading or study materials?

- Have I done all I can to find out about national initiatives and the development of the TA role and level of responsibilities? (e.g. appropriate websites.)

- Where can I find out about local courses, support and qualifications; financial help for further study; advice on career and professional development? (e.g. Local Education Authority (LEA).)

Further reading

Department for Education and Skills (2002) *Consultation on Developing the Role of School Support Staff.* London: DfES.

www.canteach.gov.uk – Teacher Training Agency's definitive website.

www.dfes.gov.uk – website for the Department for Education and Skills.

www.hlta.gov.uk – website providing easy access to up-to-date developments on higher level teaching assistant developments.

www.lg-employers.gov.uk – website providing information on the National Occupational Standards (NOS) which form the basis for National Vocational Qualifications (NVQs) at levels 2 and 3. Follow A–Z on web page, click 'T' and select relevant pages.

www.teachernet.gov.uk.

Being a Teaching Assistant

Being a teaching assistant (TA) is a difficult and demanding occupation. There are many challenges within the role itself, but in recent years these have been increased and intensified by an ever-changing set of expectations.

Having worked for several years in customer services in an international company and then raised my two children, I considered that I would make a pretty good TA. However, I have needed all my flexibility and have drawn on considerable life experience to successfully survive in the TA role. One thing I have learned is that I am always learning.

(primary TA, Honiton, Devon)

In this chapter we will:

- Consider possible explanations of why there has been an explosion in recruitment in roles supporting the teacher in our schools, the current perception of the TA role and the growth in numbers.

- Look at who are the people filling this role and what they perceive as the challenges, stresses and rewards of the position.

- Focus on a series of perceptions based on discussions with a range of contributors: how TAs see their role; how a variety of pupils see TAs and how student teachers see their future team mates.

- End with a number of perspectives on what makes a good school; offering an opportunity for TAs to assess their own work environment as it is important that TAs are supported by their school in their practice and personal and professional development.

Why has the role of teaching assistant emerged?

It is apparent that over the last 25 years there has been a change in philosophy regarding pupils with special educational needs and inclusive practice in schools and it is not a coincidence that these changes correspond to the rise in the numbers of teaching assistants.

In broad terms, up to 1981, educational thinking and process essentially segregated pupils. For example, the 1944 Education Act had defined 11 categories of handicap: blind, partially blind, deaf, partially deaf, delicate, diabetic, educationally subnormal, epileptic, maladjusted, physical disabilities and speech defects. The emphasis was strongly placed on a 'need for treatment' to provide 'remediation' to 'make children better'. This philosophy was also central to diagnosis and placement, in that pupils were assessed for placement by doctors. As a result of such assessment pupils could be labelled 'educationally subnormal', or 'severely educational subnormal' and were viewed as different from the majority. The difficulties displayed by these children were seen as a result of their disabilities, personal limitations or problems in their homes and, consequently, special help could best be provided when separate groups of students, with common problems, could be taught together. Essentially, once such groups have been provided for, the rest of the population can be educated to their assessed capabilities. Up until the 1970s further segregation was also commonly possible via a system of testing at 11. Therefore once channelled into grammar, technical, secondary modern or special schooling an appropriate ethos, curriculum, discipline structure and teachers would manage the process of education. In both the primary and secondary sectors there was thought to be little, or no need for additional, paid support in the classroom structure.

A change in thinking was signalled by the establishment of the Warnock Committee, chaired by Dame Mary Warnock. Their report in 1978 was important because it informed aspects of the 1981 Education Act which contained the first legal requirement that children with special educational needs should be integrated within mainstream schools whenever possible. Other very significant recommendations were that there should be:

- a change of emphasis from looking at the child's 'problems' to considering the child's 'needs';

- a recognition that there was a 'continuum of needs'.

In addition:

- the term special educational needs was used for the first time and,

- the committee investigated the possible number of pupils who might be experiencing such special educational needs within the school population at any one time.

They found that approximately 20% of pupils would experience difficulties at some time in their educational career. In addition, within this 20% there would be a percentage of pupils who would have difficulties that could be assessed as being so severe that they would require long-term support. The committee identified this as a group of approximately 2% who, in their opinion, would gain from having structured support through a Statement of Special Educational Need.

The subsequent legislation in 1981 drew on relatively few of the committee's recommendations. However, the importance of this report cannot be underestimated in recording a change in educational and social philosophy over disability in general and disability in education in particular. Very importantly, it meant that significantly more pupils were going to be involved in an integrated, mainstream educational system. The resultant pressure on LEAs, schools and teachers meant that some form of additional help was required in the classroom and it is from 1981 onwards that we can identify a growth in numbers of support staff in classrooms.

Although at first the recruitment was piecemeal with a range of pay, conditions and labels for the job (auxiliary welfare assistants; special needs assistants, ancillaries) gradually the title of **classroom assistant** became the norm. This title was generally replaced by **learning support assistant**, but more recently this has been usually superseded by the title of **teaching assistant**.

> The term 'teaching assistant' (TA) is the government's preferred generic term of reference for all those in paid employment in support of teachers in primary, special and secondary schools. That includes those with a general role and others with specific responsibilities for a child, subject area or age group. The term captures the essential 'active ingredient' of their work; in particular, it acknowledges the contribution which well-trained and well-managed assistants can make to the teaching and learning process and to pupil achievement.
>
> (DfEE, 2000, p. 4)

The current perception of the role

The majority of TAs are employed to fulfil specific roles, either to work closely with and provide targeted support for a pupil with identified special educational needs, or to provide a more 'general' support role in the classroom and across the school. Even in this latter role, however, the majority of time is often spent working alongside pupils who are finding aspects of learning or school life more demanding than their peers. Therefore, the role, for many, is strongly associated with providing input for pupils who have been identified as requiring additional support.

Recruitment has also been required to deliver new intitiatives such as the National Literacy and National Numeracy Strategies that advocate the use of TAs working with groups in the classroom.

How have more recent development shaped the thinking on TAs?

The 1997 Green Paper 'Excellence for all children – meeting special educational needs' signalled a rapid growth in governmental involvement and interest in the recruitment, professional development and deployment of staff supporting teachers. Since 1997, the government has acknowledged the role and value of support in documents such as 'Working with Teaching Assistants – A good practice guide' (2000); 'Professionalism and trust – the future of teachers and teaching' (2001) and 'Raising Standards and Tackling Workload – a national agreement' (2003). In addition, it has commissioned National Occupational Standards for teaching assistants (www.lg-employers.gov.uk), which have formed the basis for National Vocational Qualifications (NVQ) at NVQ levels 2 and 3, and introduced the DfES-sponsored Induction programme for new TAs.

Current and future policy is reflected in the 2002 DfES Consultation document (www.dfes.gov.uk/consultations: go to 'Archive and Results' and type in 'Support Staff'.) and changes to The Education (Teaching Work and Registration) (England) Regulations 2002.

The government recognizes the challenges ahead:

> Our schools face intense and urgent challenges. They need to progress and enrich the primary curriculum, to transform standards in secondary education, to provide more choice from 14 onwards, to tackle poor behaviour, and to respond more flexibly to the individual needs of all pupils.
>
> (DfES, 2002, Foreword)

The acknowledgement of the role and responsibilities of teaching assistants in response to these and other challenges is also recognized.

> Support staff will be critical to the achievement of these goals, both through their direct contributions and by releasing the energies of our teachers. Teaching assistants working alongside teachers have already contributed to significant improvements in the quality of teaching of literacy and numeracy. Over the coming years, we shall see further types of support staff appearing in our classrooms. That includes the development of a new stream of high level teaching assistants, pushing back the boundaries of what they can do in classrooms.
>
> (DfES, 2002, Foreword)

Consequently the government has presented a vision of the future school workforce.

> We want to unlock the full potential of the school workforce to raise standards of pupil achievement, through developing the role of support staff. With the right training and supervision, as well as sufficient numbers, support staff can release significant amounts of time for teachers and headteachers to focus on their core professional role, improving standards of teaching and learning, not being dragged back by an excessive workload of other tasks. Increased numbers of better trained support staff will in their own right enrich the experience of pupils.
>
> (DfES, 2002, p. 4)

The growth of support staff in our schools

Statistics from the Department for Education and Skills (DfES) provided the following information about support staff in schools which indicated the following trends:

In January 2002 there were 216,000 full-time equivalent support staff in schools, an increase of more than 50% since 1997. Many of these staff are part-time so the actual number of individuals will be considerably greater. The relative increases in teachers and support staff are illustrated in the graph (Fig. 1.1) below.

The graph below (Fig. 1.2) shows the way in which numbers of support staff in the categories collected in the annual schools census have changed over a five-year period. In this graph, 'TAs' includes minority ethnic support staff (bilingual language assistants) and 'other staff' includes child care staff from boarding schools, matrons/nurses and medical staff, and other uncategorized staff.

Where does the individual TA fit in to such developments?

In the Consultation of 2002, it was stated that:

> Most teaching requires the expertise and skills of a qualified teacher; but some teaching activity can be undertaken by suitably trained staff without

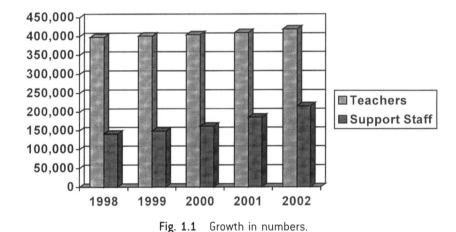

Fig. 1.1 Growth in numbers.

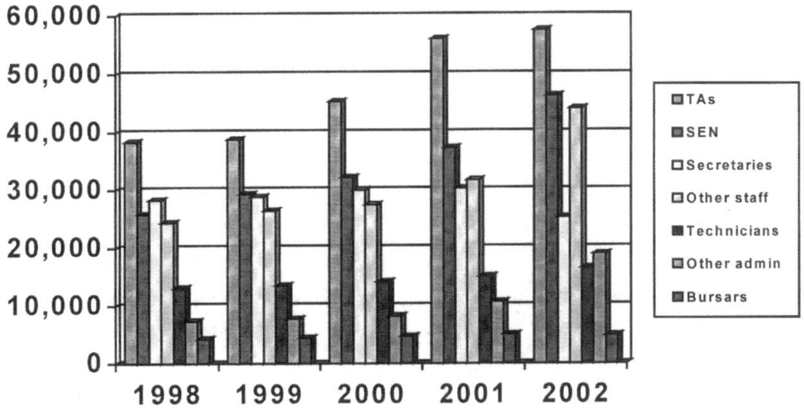

Fig. 1.2 Changing support staff roles.

QTS, provided they are working within a clear system of leadership and supervision provided by a qualified teacher. Qualified teachers must have overall responsibility for effective teaching and learning.

(DfES, 2002, p. 5)

In January 2003, local employers, most school workforce unions and the Department for Education and Skills signed a National Agreement that paved the way for radical reform of the school workforce to raise standards and tackle workload.

This Agreement included proposals to introduce the role of higher level teaching assistant (HLTA) who would bring a distinctive contribution to the work of schools. This, and other documentation sets out what is expected of those who are seeking to take on this additional responsibility including new Standards that will help to ensure that all higher level teaching assistants have the necessary skills and expertise to make an active contribution to pupils' learning. The work of HLTAs complements that of teachers and the roles are not interchangeable. HLTAs work in a range of different settings and with more autonomy than most other school support staff.

The core role of TAs is to support the pupil, the teacher, the school and the curriculum and in this role to be supported by the school.

Who are the teaching assistants required to fill such demanding expectations?

Several surveys (University of Manchester (1999), University of Southampton (1999), University of Plymouth (2002)) reveal similar factors about those filling the teaching assistants role.

Gender: 97.7% are female, 2.3% are male.

Age: as percentages:

Age	17–22	23–28	29–34	35–41	42–47	48–53	54–59	60–65
Primary	2.1%	6.0%	10.3%	33.0%	26.8%	14.2%	6.5%	1.1%
Secondary	4.3%	8.0%	9.2%	21.9%	28.5%	19.9%	7.2%	0.9%
Special	4.7%	2.8%	6.6%	31.1%	23.6%	21.8%	9.4%	0.0%

FE/HE qualifications: many may not have studied for some considerable time. In the primary sector 39.4% had no qualifications and 7.8% had or were doing a degree. In the secondary sector 34.2% had no qualifications and 17% had or were doing a degree. In special education 33.0% had no qualifications and 3.8% had or were doing a degree.

Experience: years employed as a TA as percentages:

	1 yr	2 yrs	3 yrs	4–8 yrs	9–14 yrs	15–20 yrs	21–32 yrs
Primary	26.5%	11.6%	8.7%	29.0%	18.6%	4.2%	1.4%
Secondary	34.8%	8.1%	9.5%	31.0%	13.5%	2.0%	1.1%
Special	17.9%	6.6%	7.5%	24.5%	33.0%	8.6%	1.9%

(Data from University of Plymouth survey for Department of Education and Skills, 2002. Sample of 2,500 TAs in the south west of England.)

It can be seen that most TAs in primary, secondary and special education are:

- female;

- 35+;

- over one third have been working in educational support for over four years but have not gained any post-16 qualification.

The vast majority of this hugely important and increasingly influential workforce have, from their own admission, little experience of planned and co-ordinated, accredited professional development. However, they do often share very similar emotions and aspirations. Essentially, they 'love' the job they do. It is viewed as important, rewarding, but both challenging and stressful.

The challenges/stresses and rewards of working as a TA

The teaching assistant role is an exciting experience. We know this because TAs regularly tell us so. The days are full and always different, but they do also offer a variety of challenges, stresses and rewards.

Consider the tables below produced from a selection of the identified experiences collected from many other TAs about the challenges, stresses and rewards.

Challenges

Activity

Assess the commonly identified challenges listed below against your own practice.

Challenge	Select from 1 (no challenge) to 4 (severe challenge)			
The different abilities of pupils	1	2	3	4
Retaining attention	1	2	3	4
Behaviour difficulties	1	2	3	4
Lack of 'specific' subject knowledge	1	2	3	4
Difficult parents	1	2	3	4
Limited time	1	2	3	4
Motivating disaffected pupils	1	2	3	4
Rapport with teachers	1	2	3	4
Working with supply teachers	1	2	3	4
Other:	1	2	3	4
Other:	1	2	3	4

If you can identify with these challenges then:

How do you meet them?

What skills and support do you need to overcome the most important challenges?

Who can you discuss these with, and monitor and record responses?

Stresses

Activity

Assess the following commonly identified stressors against your own practice.

Stresses	Select from 1 (no stress) to 4 (severe stress)			
Lack of resources	1	2	3	4
Poor behaviour/manners	1	2	3	4
Lack of respect	1	2	3	4
Lack of parental support	1	2	3	4
Supply teachers	1	2	3	4
Playground duties	1	2	3	4
Short notice of lesson content	1	2	3	4
Lack of planning/collaboration	1	2	3	4
Lack of space	1	2	3	4
Other:	1	2	3	4
Other:	1	2	3	4

If you can identify with these stresses then:

How do you relieve them?

What skills and support do you need to overcome the most important stresses?

This form can be photocopied. © *A Toolkit for the Effective Teaching Assistant* 2004.

Rewards

Activity

Assess the following commonly identified rewards against your own practice.

Rewards	Select from 1 (no reward) to 4 (rich rewards)			
Pupil achievement and progress	1	2	3	4
Appreciation from colleagues	1	2	3	4
Growth in confidence	1	2	3	4
Growth in knowledge of specific difficulties	1	2	3	4
Growth of self esteem amongst pupils	1	2	3	4
Growth of independence	1	2	3	4
Acceptance of your present role	1	2	3	4
Other:	1	2	3	4
Other:	1	2	3	4

If you can identify with these rewards then:

How do you build on them?

What skills and support do you need to enhance your positive development?

This form can be photocopied. © *A Toolkit for the Effective Teaching Assistant* 2004.

How do TAs see their job?

Discussions between TAs and the University of Plymouth indicate that, broadly speaking, TAs identify five specific, significant themes relating to their role and responsibilities.

Support teaching and learning

First they want to be good at their job and have the skill, knowledge and understanding to effectively support teaching and learning:

> *I want to be able to adapt the delivery of activities to be appropriate to the child I support.*
>
> (secondary TA, Truro, Cornwall)

> *My work with individual pupils with special educational needs and my groups of pupils undertaking ELS, ALS and Springboard maths means that I need to have the capabilities to provide a positive educational experience.'*
>
> (primary TA, Exeter, Devon)

An example of an HLTA Standard relevant to this theme is:

> **2.5 They know the key factors that can affect the way pupils learn.**

Within the HTLA Standards (Appendix) there are other examples that relate to teaching and learning.

Activity

On every occassion that you meet a HLTA Standard within the book, consider your own thinking and practice and reflect on these in light of that Standard.

Pastoral care and building relationships

Second, they want to be good at their job in supporting colleagues and pupils with appropriate pastoral care and building relationships.

> *I want to be able to support my teacher by opening an effective dialogue, by being a 'sounding board', by adapting to the style of teaching and providing the 3c's: collaboration, courtesy and consideration.*
>
> (primary TA, Bournemouth, Dorset)

> *I feel that I can promote confidence and positive behaviour and provide additional communication between pupil/teacher/parents/and others.*
>
> (primary TA, Okehampton, Devon)

An example of an HLTA Standard relevant to this identified theme is:

> **1.2 They build and maintain successful relationships with pupils, treat them consistently, with respect and consideration, and are concerned for their development as learners.**

Within the HLTA Standards (Appendix) there are other examples that relate to pastoral care and relationships.

Collaborative practice

> *Working together is really important to me. I can observe, support, feed back and help create a positive, stimulating environment, given the opportunity.*
>
> (secondary TA, supporting maths, Barnstaple, Devon)

An example of an HLTA Standard relevant to this third identified theme is:

> **1.4 They work collaboratively with colleagues, and carry out their roles effectively, knowing when to seek help and advice.**

Within the HLTA Standards (Appendix) there are other examples that relate to collaborative practice.

Resources and equipment

Fourth there is a realization that an essential part of that job is making certain that resources and equipment are available and of good quality.

> *I see an important part of my role as making, maintaining and utilizing resources appropriately.*
>
> (primary TA, Poole, Dorset)

An example of an HLTA Standard relevant to this identified theme is:

> **3.1.3 They contribute effectively to the selection and preparation of teaching resources that meet the diversity of pupils' needs and interests.**

Within the HLTA Standards (Appendix) there are other examples that relate to preparing resources and contributing to pupils' needs.

Future as a professional

Finally, their future as a professional within the school.

I want to be the best TA possible and this involves gaining positive insights into why children behave in certain ways, how they learn, or fail to learn and what can I do about such things apart from ask and draw on previous experience.

(secondary TA, Sherborne, Dorset)

I have found that attending good quality professional development at the appropriate level has made me far more confident in both my practice and also in discussing educational issues. It has also made me reconsider my own future and aspirations.

(primary, special school TA, Plymouth, Devon)

An example of an HLTA Standard relevant to this identified theme is:

1.6   They are able to improve their own practice, including through observation, evaluation and discussion with colleagues.

Within the HLTA Standards (Appendix) there are other examples that relate to preparing resources and contributing to pupils' needs.

Activity

Examine the five themes above and consider your own values, attitudes and beliefs about your role in school.

Evaluate your own strengths and weaknesses against each factor.

Discuss these with appropriate people in school.

Activity

Over a two-week period maintain a diary that records

(a) your support for the pupil(s);

(b) your support for the teacher(s);

(c) your support for the school;

(d) your support with the curriculum.

Activity

When you have reflected and carried out the suggested actions above then refer to the copy of the HLTA Standards in the Appendix at the end of the book.

Begin to record your conclusions against relevant Standards and begin to collect evidence from colleagues, from written work and any assessments to support your opinion for successfully attaining that Standard.

NB If you are seeking HLTA status, you should check their specific requirements for collating evidence. It may also be beneficial to contact your LEA and obviously keep your school informed.

What do pupils think about TAs?

In 2000, members of the Alliance for Inclusive Education, a young people's rights group, met at Ashwellthorpe Hall. The ages of the major contributors ranged from 9 to 18. They all attended mainstream schools and they all required support in their education.

They were asked to describe the things they liked, things they found helpful and qualities they appreciated in their TAs.

Many of the required qualities in their responses apply to the attitudes, beliefs and good practice for all TAs.

Activity

Consider the views below; evaluate them overall against your own views on the role and responsibilities of TAs and inclusive practice.

Assess your strengths and weaknesses against their criteria.

Attitudes towards TAs

Attitudes, actions and characteristics that were appreciated. Someone who was:	Self-evaluation
there for them; who liked them; 'had a big heart'; who was committed to inclusion; who would not try to be an expert but who would 'be responsive to me'.	
able to see the world from a young person's point of view.	
acting 'in loco parentis' and responsible for their safety and wellbeing at school.	
willing and open to train.	
able to spell and write clearly; able to explain difficult words; able to type and use a computer; but did not take over the teacher role for either work or discipline.	
maintained a professional relationship, guaranteeing confidentiality at all times.	
liked the other young people and could help them with their friendships.	
willing to work with other people in the class when they did not need their direct help themselves.	
a special advocate within the school, even when it meant challenging other members of staff.	

This form can be photocopied. © *A Toolkit for the Effective Teaching Assistant* 2004.

To attain such attitudes, actions and characteristics, the students felt that teaching assistants needed training in disability, equality and inclusion.

Conversely, they were all asked what they didn't like or found difficult about having TAs in mainstream school. This question made many of the young people remember events, people and attitudes which they had found very hard to deal with.

Attitudes, actions, characteristics that caused concern. Someone who was:	Self-evaluation
patronizing; shouting; talking in a high voice. This had made many of the young people angry, hurt and feeling alone.	
did things to them without asking, or responding to their needs, including having hair plaited too tightly or being left to 'roast in the sun'.	
controlling or whose attitude came between them and their friends.	
thought that they used their impairments as an excuse to get away with things, TAs who did not like them.	
was always giving up and leaving because they had 'a bad day'.	
not able to understand their school work, or did not share their interests.	
did not understand about inclusion and could not help them with their relationships with other children, under-protective, especially when they were being bullied, or over-protective and who 'ran beside me shooing away all the other children in case I ran over their feet'.	
didn't listen or really get to know them 'in a fun sense'. One person with brittle bones remembered her TA not believing her when she had broken her leg.	
could not understand the young person's speech or communication methods. One young person had had TAs who did not believe she could communicate at all – 'they think I can't think'.	
lacking in computer literacy (this was also true of some teachers).	

This form can be photocopied. © *A Toolkit for the Effective Teaching Assistant* 2004.

(Alliance for Inclusive Education, 2001)

What do trainee teachers know about TAs?

A recent informal investigation in 2004, with Year 3 students on a BEd programme, illustrated that although a small minority had experienced considerable difficulties with TAs on their weeks of practice in schools, the majority were open to exploring the role and relationship further.

Those students who had found working with TAs problematic had retained this unfortunate impression about all TAs. Their major difficulties had arisen over TAs not being prepared to listen, or not allowing them to 'take control' of the classroom.

However, the vast majority at this point in their studies had not been able to forge a relationship with a TA and had formed a vague impression of their role and responsibilities. Understandably, they had little conception of the pay and conditions for teaching assistants, but they were aware that they were now working with groups and an integral part of ELS, ALS and Springboard initiatives.

It was clear that the majority of their impressions were formed from observation, but the level of interest in how the role and responsibilities might develop and their part in relationship building was encouraging.

Schools and schooling

Overall school policies are vital to the development of practice to the work of TAs. Such policies can either foster or limit the development of effective ways of working. Schools whose policies consider the contributions of TAs have a clear view of their function.

(DfEE, 2000, p. 15)

What appears to make a good school?

Over many years schools have been examined, assessed and judged. The outcome is that certain factors seem to be important if a successful education environment is going to be created.

1 A common mission

First there needs to be a centrality of values, a clarity about what the school is about and where it is going and this needs to be 'told' by all the staff. Schools need a vision, a visible and explicit ideology. Therefore, 'a common mission'.

Activity

Assess your school against the elements of a positive 'common mission' outlined below.

Evidence of shared values and beliefs	■ values the dignity of all pupils; ■ celebrates diversity; ■ operates a zero-reject philosophy towards all pupils; ■ believes in shared responsibility and a culture of collaboration.
Clear goals	Are common goals developed by all staff? Are these recorded in a Development/Action Plan and regularly reviewed and evaluated?
Active involvement of leadership	■ supports involvement of all pupils; ■ helps with development of long-term, school-wide professional development; ■ encourages collaboration between different professionals; ■ is accessible; ■ good knowledge of pupils, staff and school; ■ acknowledges efforts and achievements of colleagues.

This form can be photocopied. © *A Toolkit for the Effective Teaching Assistant* 2004.

Vision without action is merely a dream.
Action without vision just passes the time.
Vision with action can change the world.

(Anon.)

2 *Emphasis on learning and teaching*

Second, which may sound obvious in a school, there needs to be an emphasis placed on learning and teaching which is enhanced and empowered by all staff – 'press for achievement'. All staff should have high expectations, they 'stretch' children and in turn are 'stretched' and there is mutual challenge. Therefore, 'an emphasis on learning and teaching'.

Activity

Assess your school against the elements of 'an emphasis on learning and teaching' outlined below.

Emphasis on learning	■ frequent monitoring of student behaviour;
	■ curriculum based assessment;
	■ records of achievement/profiling;
	■ combination of self-monitoring and staff assessment;
	■ rapid, explicit feedback.
High expectations	■ integrating basic skills with higher order thinking skills;
	■ all staff view themselves as teachers of basic skills;
	■ achievable expectations;
	■ positive modelling;
	■ maximizing the length of the school day.
Collegiality and development	■ good relationships;
	■ systematic, planned and appropriate use of all adults;
	■ sharing expertise;
	■ participation in professional development activities.
Instructional and curriculum focus	■ progressive, meaningful and interesting curriculum;
	■ high academic learning time;
	■ allows a variety of responses;
	■ activity-based sessions;
	■ 'authentic' experiences;
	■ variety of groupings and instructional strategies.

This form can be photocopied. © *A Toolkit for the Effective Teaching Assistant* 2004.

A learning organisation is one which facilitates the learning of all its members and continuously transforms itself.

(Pedler, Burgoyne and Boydell, 1986, p. 35)

3 A climate conducive to learning

Finally, education should be conducted in a climate that is conducive to learning. This should be based on professionalism, respect and open-two-way rapport. Professional development will help this process, but has to be seen in context of a drive for whole school improvement. Therefore, 'a climate conducive to learning'.

Activity

Assess your school against the elements of 'a climate conducive to learning' outlined below.

Parental and community involvement and support	■ inter-agency involvement;
	■ parental involvement in all aspects of school life;
	■ respect for differing cultural, linguistic and religious backgrounds.
Physical environment	■ appropriate buildings and accommodation (e.g. acoustics, accessibility)
	■ welcoming appearance;
	■ appropriate classroom layout.
Student involvement and responsibility	■ self monitoring of behaviour;
	■ responsibility for each other;
	■ involvement in the formulation of rules and regulations;
	■ giving all pupils a stake in the school.
Positive student behaviour	■ teaching social skills;
	■ respect for all;
	■ strict implementation of agreed rules and regulations.
Recognition and incentives	■ clear explanations/instructions;
	■ use of encouragement;
	■ encourage students to focus on what has been learned;
	■ opportunity for all students to participate in school-wide incentive programmes and extra-curricular activities.

This form can be photocopied. © *A Toolkit for the Effective Teaching Assistant* 2004.

What might pupils think makes a good school?

Fifteen thousand children of readers of *The Guardian* designed their perfect school in 2001. In their published manifesto it was stated:

The school we'd like	In practice this should mean
A beautiful school	Light, airy and bright.
A comfortable school	Sofas, tables that don't scrape your knees, quiet rooms.
A safe school	Swipe card entry, anti-bullying alarms, first aid classes, someone to talk to about problems.
A listening school	Children on governing body, class representatives, chance to vote for a teacher.
A flexible school	Without rigid timetables, without one-size-fits-all curriculum, chance to follow own interests.
A relevant school	Learn through experience, experiments and exploration, trips to historic sites, teachers with practical experience of what they teach.
A respectful school	Not treated as 'empty vessels' to be filled with information, treated as individuals, children and adults can talk freely to each other, opinions matter.
A school without walls	Outside to learn with animals to look after and wild gardens to explore.
A school for everybody	Boys and girls from all backgrounds and abilities, no grading, no competition, but just do your best.

At school we'd like to have

- enough pencils and books for each child;
- laptops so we could continue our work at home;
- drinking water in every classroom;
- school uniform of trainers, baseball caps, etc;
- clean toilets that don't block with paper and soap;
- fast-food school dinners and no dinner ladies;
- large lockers for storage;
- a swimming pool.

This is what we'd like it is not an impossible dream.

(The Guardian, 2001)

Activity

Carefully consider your own working environment against the theoretical model and *The Guardian* pupils' suggestions.

Are there areas where improvements could be made?

How can a school support its TAs?

Schools must recognize the importance and value of TAs and provide a thought-out, professional policy. This should take into account the different stages at which TAs are in their experience and professional development.

Initially due care and attention should be paid to the recruitment and induction of new TAs.

This should review appointment, contract terms, dialogue over job description, a proper in-school induction period and access to the DfES's induction programme.

All these processes should be open, transparent and communicated to governors and parents.

Once established in post there should be:

■ clear line management with the most appropriate line manager;

■ a continuity of work, but with regular reviews;

■ close attention to teamwork;

■ recognition of continuing professional development as vital in a positive, learning environment with the anticipation that additional study and reflection will empower the participant.

Continuing professional development will, hopefully, encourage reflection and more effective practice. However, it should be noted that the growth of knowledge, skill, understanding and confidence needs to be handled with care. Tact and diplomacy are required to initiate and maintain any worthwhile change.

> . . . the idea that you can produce, by training, a knight in shining armour who, girded with new technology and beliefs, will assault the organisational fortress and institute personal change and change in others, at a stroke. Such

a view is ingenuous. The fact of the matter is that organisations such as schools and hospitals will, like dragons, eat hero-innovators for breakfast.

(Georgiardes and Phillimore, 1975, p. 315)

As a final activity, having read and hopefully engaged in the activities and reflective process in the chapter, I suggest that you examine and discuss your own, existing job description in the light of any new perceptions.

Activity

Consider your job descriptions.

If you do not have a job description, or you believe it to be dated, then draw on your reflections from the Activities in this chapter to re-examine what you do and open a dialogue.

Summary

This chapter recognizes the growth in numbers of teaching assistants and tries to provide a rationale for this phenomenon. Recruitment has been accompanied by changes in role, responsibilities and exceptions. It provides an opportunity for TAs to reflect on their philosophies and practice against preceptions of other TAs, and a range of additional sources.

Further reading

DfEE (2000) *Working with Teaching Assistants*. London: DfEE.
www.htla.gov.uk
www.teachernet.gov.uk

Understanding Change and Being an Integral Part of the Process

Aims

Reading this chapter and undertaking some or all of the tasks provides an opportunity to consider a phenomenon, 'change', that might be seen as abstract, but which affects so much, if not all, that we all do in schools. We live in a society of perpetual change and this is reflected in the world of education. Within this, the role, responsibilities and status of your professional group, teaching assistants (TAs), constantly seems subject to development and change, never more so than through the current restructuring of the workforce.

This chapter will help you consider change in your workplace from a variety of perspectives, including those changes which:

- are **imposed on the school** by local or national government agencies. This assumes that: you are party to change that is created and administered by others; you are not involved in the drive for change and it is done *to you*;

- are **part of the school** and which may or may not influence your working life in school. This assumes that: you are part of a team that is developing and managing change, so it is done *with you*;

- are part of **your own professional development**. This assumes that: you are a change agent in your own right in that you take a leading part in the creation of the change, how it is carried out and how it is maintained and monitored. You are the 'driver' of the change and, therefore, it is done *by you*.

The notion of the TA as **a leader of change** has been brought into sharper focus with the advent of Higher Level Teaching Assistants (HLTA) status, the introduction of Standards and other workforce reforms that are taking place in schools.

This chapter will help you to examine the process of change and to understand it, deal with it and, perhaps, lead it. It assumes we live in a world of rapid change in education and it also assumes a positive approach to it, or at least acknowledges that:

there is a certain relief in change, even though it be from bad to worse . . . it is often a comfort to shift one's position and be bruised in a new place.

(Washington Irving, *Tales of a Traveller*, 1824).

Change is often associated with management in education and, therefore, might seem more to do with dealing with systems and less to do with the day to day work of teaching assistants. However, even if not leading change, evolving patterns of work mean that TAs are being drawn into increased involvement and decision making in schools. The developing roles and responsibilities of TAs, mentioned by Richard Tyrer in the previous chapter, mean that in many cases TAs are not just passive observers, but contributors and innovators in their own right. This chapter is about ideas and practices that might support such new roles.

If change is to be effective it must address and have an impact on the values of staff in schools. These do not change overnight and that is why it is rare for effective change to take place speedily, especially if it clashes with the values of staff, particularly those in senior positions.

To be successful it needs to resonate with a 'critical mass' of both teachers and TAs, (the 'common mission' of Chapter 1) which suggests that much 'top-down' change will need to be adapted to fit the values of particular schools or is likely to be superficially incorporated, even rejected. All change that is badly handled will be damaging, as Fullan (1993, p. 59) states:

> clumsy or superficial attempts at reform, actually decrease commitment – they make matters worse.

Recently while standing in an art gallery I looked at a painting, a fairly traditional portrait, and my mind wandered around the idea that portrait paintings could be construed as a metaphor for change in education. This is the path that the meanderings followed.

Change in education is continuous, endemic, part of the world of schools. Perhaps it has always been the case but, somehow, in the modern school system, the quantity of change seems to be ever increasing. There are several forces that drive change and they include those which are:

- ■ part of modern society, our civilisation – this is the canvas;

- ■ part of the political agenda of our time – this is the frame;

- ■ part of our institutional agenda for change – this is the background;

- ■ our personal need to make a difference and be a change agent, such as the need to help children with learning difficulties, or part of a change that we deem as necessary in our school or classroom – this is the most important part, the subject.

First, let us consider those changes that are happening in society, seemingly not in our control. These are often to do with the values that we claim to embrace as a society and the means by which we gather information and communicate. For example, witness the changes in our notions of the family, or how we have come to embrace computer technology in so many areas of our life, including the classroom. They, like a canvas, are the backcloth, the context in which change will be delivered.

Second, there are those changes that are imposed from above (see Fig. 2.1 below). These are largely determined by the policy makers whose main objectives are to realize promised targets to the electorate, to create the workforce that will maintain their ideas of an economy, to be better than other countries and to be re-elected! In the UK this is through the government organs such as the Department for Education and Skills (DfES) and the Teacher Training Agency (TTA) who generate reforms – for example creativity in the curriculum, Standards for TAs – all designed to raise standards by transferring a particular version of the truth to schools. These often manifest themselves in another

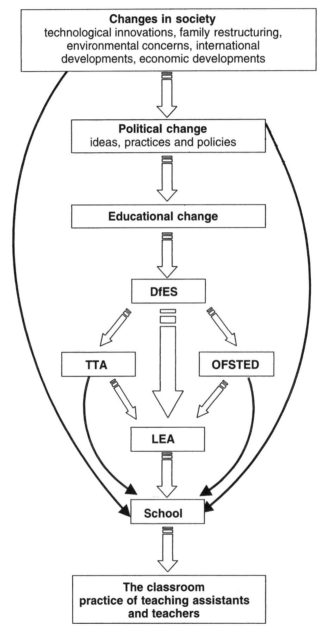

Fig.2.1   Changes imposed on classroom practice.

layer, the local initiatives through the LEA, sometimes reacting to the central government view and, occasionally, having the temerity to generate initiatives that respond to local needs. These are the frame in which the painting is set and they are subject to being changed themselves. Often these forces seem far removed from the classroom situation and the world of teaching assistants, but the reform agenda seems unremitting and ever prevalent. Its focus often appears to be on what is wrong with schools and instant correction, rather than nurturing sustained positive attitudes and informed ideas towards creating the schools of tomorrow.

Governmental forces for change, be they national or local, bear down upon schools themselves, which in turn form the third type of change. They are cultures that need or demand change, expressed through their 'Development Plan' or the new headteacher keen to make their mark, or a new head of department full of drive and initiatives, seeking to set up a variety of enterprising programmes. They provide the essential background element which does much to set the tone and influence how the final picture looks.

In turn, all these forces press their needs, requests and ideas on individuals in the classroom – teaching assistants and teachers and the children who are the centre of their attention, industry and skills.

TAs and the teachers with whom they work will also want to bring change to their classrooms and this may sometimes seem less important than that which forms part of the agendas of others. *This is not the case* for the deliverers of change, i.e. the people in the classroom, are the centre of the picture, the subject of the painting, the means by which the education of children is delivered and achieved. Of course, the painting is enhanced by quality canvas, the frame, the background and the setting, but the *subject provides the focus* and, more than any other element, will determine its success as a painting.

Sometimes, maybe many times, the idea of the people working in classrooms being central does not appear to be the case, but, to be successful, education still demands personal ideas, skills and philosophies delivered by adults in the school. As Fullan (1993, p. 39) reminds us:

> change is too important to leave to the experts.

This chapter is written with the notion that you, the teaching assistant, are *a significant adult* in the lives of many children and your colleagues, the working of your school and that you are an agent for change, either in your own right or alongside others who work with you.

This being the case it seemed that any book looking at the world of the teaching assistant should contain a chance to read, stand back and reflect on the phenomenon that we call change.

Activity

Consider a recent change that you were involved in at your school or in your classroom (or a recent school or classroom in which you worked) and record your responses to these questions.

1   Was the change generated by national government agencies, local government, the senior managers of the school, teachers or teaching assistants or other sources?

2   Who, in the school, supported the change and was there resistance?

3   What was your stance – were you in favour of it, against it or neutral towards it? (List the good and not so good points that it possessed.)

4   What has been the outcome of the change in terms of (a) how people behave (b) their attitudes and values?

5   Does the origin of a change, i.e. who or what generated it, affect how you view it and your desire to be involved?

The nature of change

Before discussing practical matters it is important to look at what change is and reflect on some key features that will apply to most changes. Change is about people behaving differently and, at its most effective, it will also be about changing attitudes and values. Remember too that change means to make different or to alter – it does not necessarily mean to improve or make better. Consider, especially if you are leading change or involved as a 'driver' of the change, that not everyone may think that it is a good idea – they may be right about it or they could fear having to learn or do new things. Change is often about making a difference to something that already exists rather than radical reorganization of the fundamentals – it is then more about amending or adjusting, not transforming.

The innovation fatigue that schools seem to experience often compels them to amend, rather than reflect on, the fundamentals of what they are doing.

For example, many schools review their behaviour policy in the light of what they perceive to be falling standards in the behaviour of their pupils. The first ports of call are usually sanctions and rewards and how they can be more effective. Rarely do they start by asking:

- **Why do we believe that standards of behaviour are getting worse?** Ways of behaving are constantly changing as are the ways that society responds to that behaviour. One or two key incidents can lead to reaction that demands change when, perhaps, it is not needed or there is a need to look at what is causing a pupil to behave in a certain way and deal with that fundamental problem before resorting to sanctions.

■ **What kind of school do we want to create?** All adults will play a part in contributing to the culture of the school, although few are often involved in generating what is often described as the 'vision'. This does not prevent us from having our own vision and ideas about the kind of school we are working towards or want to maintain.

■ **What expectations do we have of our pupils**? Do we set high expectations for all pupils, not just concerning learning, but also behaviour?

■ **How does this link with our behaviour and that of the pupils?** We often forget our role in contributing to pupils' behaviour, not just as a role model, but also in the way that we deal with them. Often teaching assistants feel compelled to react differently to pupils, especially ones with whom they work closely, or they develop slightly different relationships than the teachers.

■ **Why not approach the issue from an alternative position and have a 'positive relationships' policy?** Would not part of the vision that we have for our pupils be to help them to create positive relationships both now and in the future? This approach is inclusive of all pupils, not just those who commit misdemeanours.

The ownership of change is so important and with change imposed on schools from outside forces it often means that staff within them are forced to react without understanding or valuing what has been proposed and, therefore, lacks a creative element and has no sense of responding to needs identified from within. It may alter the system, but it has less chance of stirring hearts and minds.

> Change comes from small initiatives which work, initiatives which, imitated, become fashion. We cannot wait for great visions from great people, for they are in short supply at the end of history. It is up to us to light our own small fires in the darkness.
>
> (Handy, 1994)

Change is, therefore, often incremental and depends upon several small moves forward or opportunities, not giant leaps.

Attitude to change

Whatever your own role it is likely that you will encounter different attitudes to a particular change from individuals and, in the case of larger schools, groups. There will be those who are totally against it and will be negative, even aggressive (Busher, 2001, p. 90), **active resisters**. There will also be those who, whilst opposing the change, understand why it is taking place, and may do little to oppose it, **passive resisters**. Similar to that group are those who are prepared to **try everything**. They do not care or do not want to be involved in the management of the change, indeed, at times they may appear to be neutral about the whole process. Often this is the case if they are not directly affected by what is happening, but this attitude changes when the full implications are known or they become personally involved. There are those who are **change followers** of most changes and support them, often believing that there is an inevitability about it or that resistance may be a waste of energy. Finally, there is a group that responds positively to change, the **change drivers**, who do so in the early stages, but become somewhat less enthusiastic during the stages when it is less innovative and more hard work. All these groups, in themselves, can change in composition and you might recognize yourself in more than one role.

Activity

Consider the changes mentioned in the left-hand column below.

What is/was your attitude to them?

Put a tick in the column that best matches your attitude i.e. Active Resister (AR), Passive Resister (PR), Try Everything (TE), Change Follower (CF) or Change Driver (CD).

You may find that you want to tick more than one column, as you have changed in attitude, or that none of the descriptions matches your views (how would you describe your attitude?).

In the case of the first four you may also find that a specific change does not apply to your school and that your answer will be theoretical.

Change	AR	PR	TE	CF	CD
Changing titles from learning support or classroom assistant to teaching assistant in your school					
Teaching assistants studying Foundation degrees					
The development of the Standards for higher level teaching assistants					
The National Numeracy Strategy					
Introducing more creativity into the curriculum					
Extensive training for Mealtime Assistants (MTAs)					
Teaching assistants taking a more active role in teaching groups and classes					
An imaginary one (or is it?). The abolition of exclusion from school!					
Teaching citizenship as a subject					
A recent change at your school e.g. . . .					

This form can be photocopied. © *A Toolkit for the Effective Teaching Assistant* 2004.

Just as individuals have an approach to change so do schools, and not all schools embrace change and not all are good at it. Those which are good at change have certain characteristics and these can summarized by two words: **communication** and **teamwork**. Those which are not so good, who may well be operating at what Everard and Morris describe as 'dynamic conservation' which maintains the current structures and familiarity, as change is threatening.

Fullan (1982) discovered four groups amongst teachers in attitude to change:

- ■ a minority who said leave us alone, we will get on with it ourselves;

- ■ a minority who did not want to write policies but were prepared to resource them and be involved in decision making;

- ■ a majority who were prepared to have materials made for them and did not have the time for decision making;

- ■ an equal majority who saw time as a problem but wanted to be involved at all levels and share ideas with fellow professionals.

Activity

Do the above categories apply to TAs?

In the various teams e.g. classroom teams, TA teams, subject teams, are there groups who have developed positive or negative attitudes to change?

How would you describe these groups?

Whatever disadvantages there are in people not agreeing with or sharing your enthusiasm for change Fullan (1993) points out that there are also dangers in everyone agreeing with what is happening – '**groupthink**.'

Collaboration may not always be a positive force and it is important that dissent or differing views are heard. Certainly collaboration does not necessarily bring consensus. How often has practice in the classroom been enhanced by teaching assistants questioning and debating the practice of their teacher colleagues – and vice versa! When staff go along with a request from administrative or central bodies, or when there is majority for a certain position, it does not mean that the decision is wise and will lead to good practice. Positive conflict asks us to question and use professional judgment to determine if there are benefits and deficits in a particular idea, without hurting or offending others. Such a process is also a healthy model for pupils.

Activity

Consider how evident the following are in your professional relationships with those with whom you are likely to be involved in change. Do you:

1　Agree to disagree? (indeed it is established that disagreement is legitimate and that sometimes this will manifest itself with high emotion. Education should arouse passion, feelings and differences in values, attitudes and practices.)

2　Maintain a sense of humour, avoid cornering someone who has a different view to your own and avoid reacting to unintentional remarks?

3　Deal with one issue at a time, while maintaining an eye on the 'big picture' and avoid solutions that come too easily or quickly?

4　Focus on what people want and not why they want it?

A second cautionary term, and one whose meaning is often recognized by teaching assistants, is **balkanization**. This refers to a situation in which members of a group develop loyalties which are so strong that they fail to empathize with other groups, ignore them or even become hostile towards them. In some schools teaching assistants are seen as a separate group whose identity is totally distinct from other staff in schools, to the point where they even have their own staffrooms! Mary Pittman, in the chapter on teamwork, mentions the negativity felt by some teaching assistants who felt like the 'spy in the classroom' and 'overgrown pupils'. Despite the differences between teachers and teaching assistants in pay and conditions, they have more in common than separates them. Meeting the needs of the pupils, fulfilling the aspirations of the school summarized in the development plan and playing an active role in a positive dynamic culture are all common aspirations and far outweigh the differences in the two 'camps'.

Problems with the 'system'

It is not only the willingness or the attitude of your colleagues that will determine whether change can be implemented, but the school itself may have problems within it. For example, this has much to do with how it has been managed, or its history in generating innovation or taking ideas on board, or its relationship with the wider community. These factors might be described as the '**system**'. Murgatroyd and Morgan (1993) drew up Senge's 'Archetypes of Systems' (1990) and noted that systems can facilitate change or can possess inhibitors to change and one or more of these might be in your school system. Most TAs will identify one or two of the following issues, but they become more problematic if they are part of the system and its response to change.

They include:

- The need to **balance the process of change with delay**. Moving too quickly or over reacting with a desire to adopt a specific innovation can create a feeling of dissatisfaction and turbulence from some groups. In the end, the negativity generated causes more problems and takes up more time than the initial problem.

- There may be **limits to growth** and development in the school. A school becomes successful, consequently, pupil numbers and class sizes increase with pressure being brought to expand and employ more TAs, who are not as motivated and as well trained as the others. The very quality and teamwork of the TAs that made the school successful cannot be sustained and quality suffers with a resulting decline in numbers. Few good TAs want to work there.

- **Shifting the burden** to a quick fix sudden solution, such as buying a new mathematics scheme to counter poor SATs results or employing three new TAs to deal with behaviour problems, which were a result of poor practice and policy in behaviour management.

- **Shifting the burden to an outside intervenor** by calling in an expert such as the Educational Psychologist and expecting her/him to come up with a magic solution to dealing with 'Albert'. Another intervener is the professional development day with an outside speaker who makes an impassioned plea for staff to take on board the 'new' thinking on, say, multiple intelligences. Everyone agrees it was a great session and it is assumed that messages included will happen – just like that! Such ideas need personalizing to the school and its staff and it is that which brings genuine change, however inspiring or amusing the speaker was.

- Schools **erode the goals** and settle for a change that was not as ambitious as the original aspiration. For example, the new mathematics scheme appears to work well, so changes in that area need go no further or plans to employ four new skilled TAs are abandoned despite the preparation work having been undertaken and staff promised increased support.

- Successful change becomes identified with one person, who is perceived as a winner and will receive funding and accolades. By implication there are losers, whose attitude to the laudable innovation is scarred by the process adopted within the system. They adopt a negative stance and the conflict assumes an **escalation**.

- Similar to the above **more success goes to the successful**. For example, the new reading scheme is a big hit with some staff, therefore it is developed further at the expense of other areas of the curriculum.

- Alternatively there may be **growth and under-investment** and early success is not maintained as a plan for new investment does not materialize. This does not only apply to financial under investment but also to precious staff skills.

■ Staff chase resources at the time of announced budget restraint and there is a panic demand, inability to prioritize and the resource allocation becomes unmanageable, leading to everyone feeling disenfranchized and aware that senior managers cannot manage resources. Senge (1990) referred to this as **tragedy of the commons**.

■ **Fixes that fail** appear to happen a great deal. Albert's behaviour has become so bad that there is no option but the often used exclusion process. Before long another pupil emerges as the cause of the main behaviour problem, exclusion is considered again without any reflection on behaviour management in the school, resulting in the burden of the school not being lightened.

Activity

Consider the problems identified above. Look at one which appears to be relevant to your situation (if there is not one select a problem that you have had experience of or could foresee happening).

(a) Using Forcefield Analysis (p. 43) examine how you might begin the process of changing the system.

(b) Consider the role that TAs can bring in determining the approaches within school systems as well as individual pupil learning.

As a leader of change

It may be an expectation that the headteacher is a leader of change, but an unusual role for a teaching assistant, yet increasingly school leaders are looking to their staff to be innovative and to play a major role in school development. Here are some principles that might help to inform your role as a change agent. They include that:

■ you will have little idea how things will work out in the end;

■ the culture of the school, including the systems, and the ways that people are treated will be significant;

■ there will be numerous approaches to achieving the required change and some of those will bring 'turbulence', which has been defined as: 'change that accelerates faster than our capacity to keep pace with it' (Whitaker, 1998, p. 13);

■ the commitment of others as support may not be necessary at the beginnings of a change project, but you will need support as the process gathers pace and, more importantly, if you are to achieve the desired outcome;

- there will be unexpected support from some people and opposition from those whom you predicted would support the ideas;

- conflict is likely to form part of the process, and this will be expected by many participants. As mentioned previously, not all conflict is counter-productive.

One caution here is that it is often the case that change leaders are seen charging ahead with change in a solitary manner, they are perceived to be, as mentioned in Chapter 1, the 'Hero Innovator'. School staff who attend courses, or undertake research, are often greeted with statements such as 'we can tell you have been on a course' when they come to introduce a practical innovation that has fired their interest and they have perceived the relevance to the school. It is vital to recognize that *it is the innovation, not the innovator, that is more significant* and it is important to plan and involve others. Identify, consult and work with the supportive forces in the school, the 'critical mass' that will be the sustaining team.

They:

- may not always be at the top of an organization, but may be near to it;

- may be the people who have the will, resources or freedom to manage operations;

- will help you to frequently revisit the issue and check all is going well as monitoring will be essential.

It is highly unlikely that a great deal will be achieved without the consent and support of those near the top of the organization and more will be achieved if they are active in their backing of the process. Fullan (1993, in Everard) suggests that 'neither centralization nor decentralization works' and that both forces that operate 'top-down' and those which operate 'bottom-up' will be required if the change is to be realized.

Tools to aid planning change

Planning any change allows opportunities to reflect upon change direction and how it will be achieved. The benefits of even limited planning outweigh the small amount of time required and help to identify the likely sources of support and opposition. Innovation brought about by sudden action and little planning has less change of making a genuine change to practice. One aid to planning is Forcefield Analysis which is premised on the idea that not everyone thinks an innovation is a good idea, and there will be both support and opposition. It makes explicit that feelings are an important factor in a change. Forcefield Analysis is an aid to planning as it provides a vehicle that:

(a) compels reflection upon the change that you want to make. We often find that we have been involved in a change or led a change that does not match what we actually wanted to achieve;

(b) asks you to consider the areas – the 'forces' – that will provide support and facilitate the change. These are important in that allies and supportive systems will help facilitate, motivate and maintain the impetus;

(c) asks you to consider the 'forces' that will counter the change or, at least, will not facilitate it. On first identification of these forces it seems that these are nothing more than problems, but they are important for they compel examination of the change and they remind us that problems are inevitable and that we learn from them;

(d) helps planning by asking you to 'measure' the size of both sets of forces and then consider which will make the best allies and which forces need to be countered or confronted first.

Activity

Forcefield Analysis

1   Draw your own copy of the template of the Forcefield provided below. Consider a change that you are involved in at your school, either as leader, a member of a team or by yourself. If you cannot easily think of one then try one of the selections in the Activity on attitudes to change (above). Write down *exactly* what change you wish to see in the box provided.

2   List the key areas of support – they may be people, but they can also be other forms of resource (time, income, legislation).

3   List the key forces that will prove difficult, obstruct or counter the change.

4   In the box at the end of each arrow give each supporting and countering force a number from 1 to 5 in accordance with their significance. For example, the main agent that supports the change will be a 5 and a less significant, but still supportive agent, may be a 1 or 2. Similarly, the main agent that counters the change will be a 5 and a less significant, but still negative agent, may be a 1 or 2.

5   Consider the positive forces and which ones might help in overcoming the barriers – they may have a specific area that they can overcome. How best can they be brought into play?

6   Consider the negative forces and which ones might inhibit the movement of the change. The question that presents itself here is usually should we go for the highest number barrier, hoping that it will influence the lesser forces or should we achieve an initial small success that motivates further movement? It feels a little like a military plan, but it helps to provide the chance to reflect and plan before moving to action. It also will help to identify those things which cannot be changed.

What change do you wish to bring about?

Forcefield   ....

Analysis   ....

Countering Forces

Direction of
change

Supportive Forces

Opposition to change

Sometimes the opponents of specific change raise their objections openly, offering reasons, perhaps excuses, why they cannot sanction what is happening. These include such ideas as:

- the teaching staff will oppose this;

- it does not match the school policy on . . .;

- we don't have the resources (time, skill, money);

- it won't work in this school (too big, too small, specialist role e.g. special school);

- we are drowning in changes as it is;

- it is just another fad;

- it won't help us overcome our main problems which are . . .;

- it won't help me to do my job better;

- we have done it all before, except last time we called it . . .;

- please, not before the Ofsted inspection!

If they are reasons they may be valid, and compel revisiting the plan – but not abandoning the change project itself. Think about the times you have used these yourself and with justification!

However, if they are excuses, e.g. Ofsted are not visiting in the near future, and anyway, the changes are in line with the last action plan, then move ahead in the knowledge that you know who will oppose or, at least, not support, and why.

The main goal, as Rodd (1994, p. 122) suggests, is to ensure that staff express their fears and worries to you and to each other, rendering subterfuge unlikely. The real danger may be those who say they will be behind you and when you look back you cannot see them!

No one likes to think that people oppose their ideas or changes that they see as valuable or necessary, but it is hardly likely that everyone will support you in an idea that you have. The resisters, whether active or passive, force us to ask important questions about the nature of the idea, its value and how we might introduce it. They can be seen as healthy conflict and part of the change process for which you have planned and on which you will reflect. Controversy follows innovation and the greater the threat to current practice the more extensive and intensive the opposition is likely to be.

They may even be right! An example of what looks at first sight to be quite controversial is not blaming or punishing bullies in school. When explained as not a 'soft option', that it will involve positive approaches to the victim of bullying and that it means the bully has to change their behaviour, rather than make sure they are not caught next time, then it appears less controversial. However, it does cause opposition in schools if introduced.

Not all opposition is helpful and constructive, indeed, it may be that there is a deliberate attempt to undermine the change by adopting tactics that seek to destroy or deflect or they assume a powerless, negative stance that has the same effect – it counters the change. You may well recognize these 'characters' from your experience, they:

- appear reasonable and seem to be approving but then offer a series of 'yes but' statements, which has the effect of closing conversation as they really mean 'no';

- spot a mistake or blemish in the proposal documentation and raise it to undermine the impact of your idea;

- demonstrate considerable skill in waiting for the mistake, even misleading or trapping you into making it, and then they pounce;

- appear in favour but their presence is more to do with personal aggrandisement and promotion than genuine support for change;

- have far too much to do to be bothered with your ideas and the idea becomes immediately downgraded. Occasionally they take on too much by choice and justify not coping and contributing by saying that they are suffering with over-work;

- resort to a problem they have or a lack of status and influence. They don't see that they can make a contribution. It may be nervousness around an issue or perceived lack of training that prevents them joining the team;

- set themselves up to fail and appear to be a victim of the challenges presented by the change;

- blame your idea for their own inability to manage their time and complete other tasks.

Activity

Consider the negative 'characters' mentioned above through the following questions:

- are these recognizable to you?

- can they be involved or, perhaps more importantly, can you afford to leave them out of a change?

- how might they best be involved?

- do you recognize yourself?

Another aid to planning change is a SWOT analysis. This can be used as a tool to interrogate the **value** of the change as well as **how it will be achieved** within a school. It requires a consideration of four aspects:

Strengths: what are the main strengths of the idea?
Weaknesses: what weaknesses can be predicted?
Opportunities: what opportunities might be presented by it?
Threats: what might be the threats that it brings?

Activity

Using a SWOT analysis (example below)

Let us consider a change that might be seen in today's schools as outrageous or impractical: the abolition of exclusion of pupils. While it may seem far fetched, it is important to consider that many other ideas have seemed outrageous at one time or another but are now part of everyday life in schools, e.g. the abolition of corporal punishment, the use of computers in schools, the National Curriculum and, more pertinently, the extensive deployment of teaching assistants, many of whom are studying Foundation degrees and are highly qualified and experienced. In small groups or individually, use copies of the SWOT grid provided to answer the following:

■   what are the main strengths of abolishing exclusion?

■   what are the weaknesses of the idea?

■   what opportunities might be presented by such a change?

■   what threats does it bring?

If you have worked in a group, reconvene and consider:

(a) whether there is consensus;

(b) if the SWOT analysis has brought about a change in thinking in some people;

(c) if it is worth considering.

If so, look at the Forcefield Analysis as a way of planning the next step.

Strengths	Weaknesses
Opportunities	Threats

This form can be photocopied. © *A Toolkit for the Effective Teaching Assistant* 2004.

In the world of rapid development that is the modern school, change, more than ever, should have an aim and a purpose. It is important to avoid an overload of new ideas, but the context of the school development is significant. It therefore needs to be viable in terms of time, as well as the disposition and skills of the staff. All too often great ideas become lost in a swamp of innovation.

It is important to reflect on an idea or innovation and begin to plan what will happen and who will be involved. Here are some final ideas designed to help the planning and process of change.

1   During the initial stages avoid organizing too much and getting involved in minutiae. Detailed structures and procedures are likely to be developed during the process and not at the outset.
2   Similarly, avoid simple solutions as they are likely to be limited in their scope, partial in their achievement and probably wrong!
3   Select people who will support you and who will be interested in, but not necessarily in agreement with, in what you are doing.
4   Examine the negatives, and consider that the forces that run counter to an innovation need to be heard and their contribution considered.
5   By communicating with others at all levels, in all ways, and like never before, uncertainty, fear and rumour are reduced and the perception of threat may turn into opportunity.

In the end, more will be achieved by a planned innovation that proves rewarding for the team involved than any imposed change led by an individual, especially an outsider. Therefore, before you read about how teams work and how they facilitate good practice in the next chapter, consider the merits of a team approach to change in which decision-making is shared work and commitment gained through the early involvement of others. Remember that change is not a single event, even a series of events, it is a journey, with hidden dangers, unknown outcomes and pleasant surprises. We might learn to fear change less for as I am told Buddhists say:

> . . . all suffering of mankind is produced by attachment to a previous
> condition of existence. When we eliminate our expectations as to how the
> future ought to be a continuation of the past, we guarantee ourselves more
> peace of mind.

Summary

This chapter suggests that you take an active role in schools and are increasingly involved as agents of change. Teaching assistants are invited to look at their attitude to change and to consider how changes can be planned and supported.

Further reading

Everard, K. and Morris, G. (1996) *Effective School Management* (3rd ed). London: Paul Chapman.

Fullan, M. (1993) *Change Forces: Probing the Depths of Educational Reform.* London: Falmer Press.

Whitaker, P. (1998) *Managing Schools.* Oxford: Butterworth.

TAs and Teachers Working Together: Collaborative and Supportive Partnerships

Teachers and teaching assistants (TAs) working alongside each other to raise standards and maximize potential is now an aspect of life in most schools. Under the government's new proposals (2002) this partnership is set to become more formalized and continue to undergo change in the development of roles, responsibilities and working partnerships.

Such working partnerships can be very effective and, as a consequence, be beneficial for pupils and schools. However sometimes the partnership between teachers and teaching assistants can be a frustrating experience for both and this potentially decreases the impact for pupils and produces stress for one or both parties.

This chapter aims to allow the reader to:

- evaluate personal and professional strengths and weaknesses;

- reflect on the meaning and values of working together;

- encourage communication within a professional framework;

- empower the working partnership within positive teamwork structures.

An example of an HLTA Standard relevant to this theme is:

> **1.4   They work collaboratively with colleagues and carry out their roles effectively, knowing when to seek help and advice.**

There are examples of other Standards that relate to collaborative working and supportive partnership throughout this chapter and in the Appendix. At each such occasion the reader can reflect on their own practice in working together.

Defining teamwork and partnership practice

What does 'teacher and TA partnership' or 'teamwork' mean?
An existing definition of this relationship states that:

> a team is a group in which the individuals have a common aim and in which
> the jobs and skills of each member fit in with those of others, as . . . in a jigsaw
> puzzle pieces fit together without distortion and together produce an overall
> pattern.
>
> (Babington, Smith and Farrell (1979) cited in Lacey (2001 p. 36))

This chapter asks you to reflect upon your own setting and evaluate how close your working
teacher/TA relationship is to 'a well-constructed jig-saw' as suggested by Babington et al.

As you begin to think about this vital partnership, share your thoughts with a teacher
or teachers and discuss your underlying beliefs about your working practice.

- What works very well?

- What works satisfactorily?

- What areas could be improved?

It should be recognized that working with other adults in the demanding atmosphere of
a classroom can present personal and professional hurdles that need to be **acknowledged, addressed and overcome**. In any successful relationship, there has to be
understanding, compromise and empathy.

The roles and responsibilities of TAs have changed dramatically over the last ten years,
however, there is a clear starting point for the teacher/TA relationship, emphasized
recently in the Teacher Training Agency (TTA) Consultation, namely:

> Only qualified teachers can take overall responsibility and accountability for
> the quality and outcomes of teaching and learning.
>
> (TTA, 2002, p. 14)

The teacher, therefore, is the **manager** in the classroom. However, as part of their
managerial responsibility teachers need to recognize that TAs also have increasingly
clear and distinct responsibilities which must be realized and effectively co-ordinated to
ensure that roles are complementary and provide the most effective support for pupils.

Tilstone, Lacey et al (2000) recognize some of the complex issues facing teachers and
schools in collaborating with teaching assistants and consider the difficulties of equality
in terms of status, pay and conditions:

> there is a fine line to be drawn between exploiting this group of staff and
> properly involving them in the pupils' learning.

Balshaw (1999, p. 12) provides some comments from TAs which show how they can sometimes feel when they are not considered as part of a team:

■ 'piggies in the middle'

■ 'in no-man's land'

■ 'dogsbodies'

■ 'spy in the classroom'

■ 'overgrown pupils'

■ 'left up in the air'.

To support this, on the same page, she provides six principles required to produce a successful collaborative school environment that embraces TAs. These are:

■ clear and defined roles and responsibilities;

■ good communication;

■ consistency of approach;

■ a working team;

■ personal and professional skills;

■ staff development needs.

Key factors that reinforce the value of TAs

During my own research discussions with TAs I have discovered that there appear to be five key factors that continually emerge which provide TAs with a feeling that they are valued and reassured that they are making a positive contribution to their school and to the classroom environment in which they work.

TAs suggested that from their perspective good practice included:

(a) having 'active' systems of providing and accessing information;

(b) opportunities created for 'talk time' between teachers and TAs;

(c) an ethos of collaboration and inclusion in planning about pupil learning;

(d) a recognition and encouragement of the part played by TAs in differentiating work for pupils;

(e) communication between teachers and TAs which encouraged a shared perspective on understanding pupil needs.

In this chapter activities are presented that relate to these five key factors. The activities aim to provide a basis for **reflection on practice** and can be carried out individually by TAs; by TAs and teachers together; or TAs and other members of the senior management team in order to evaluate collaborative practices and develop ideas, strategies and teamwork still further. Examples which draw on the positive feedback provided by experienced TAs on the Foundation degree programme are included to simply provide a guide, or source of starter ideas, and allow the natural creativity in schools to promote even more collaborative and supportive practice between teachers and TAs.

(a) 'Active' systems of information

It can be difficult for TAs to get the information they need to feel fully part of a team or to feel valued in a partnership. It can equally be difficult for teachers to have the time to ensure that they have kept the assistant up to date with all the factors relating to the school, department, class and individual pupils.

An example of an HLTA Standard relevant to this theme is:

> **1.6   They are able to improve their own practice, including through observation, evaluation, and discussion with colleagues.**

Within the HLTA Standards (Appendix) there are other examples that relate to professional values and practice.

The example below provides a variety of sources of information that some TAs have suggested would be useful to them, as well as ways in which various schools have set about providing good communication of information.

From observations in schools and discussions with teachers and TAs it is apparent that information is prioritized and communicated at different 'levels', and in different directions. Clearly, schools need to be managed and not all information should be, or needs to be, in the public domain; for example certain sensitive information about pupils. However the communication system should apply to the whole school; offer the capacity for appropriate staff access; the opportunity to interpret the content and its value; to provide, if required, a channel for responding, regular review and if necessary, updating.

Consider the activity below in reviewing what systems of information are already in place and what systems TAs and other staff would like to find in place in the school.

Activity

Use the categories listed in the reflective activity column, below (or draw on your own experiences, as is appropriate to your setting) to assess the active systems of information in your school.

Identify what systems already exist for providing you, in your TA role, with the information sources required to be most effective.

Consider ways to further develop active information sources in your work setting. Teaching colleagues could also do this exercise and information could then be pooled and discussed.

This will help TAs to evaluate what information they think they need to carry out their role effectively and could give senior managers and teachers the opportunity to evaluate their current information systems.

Reflective activity: Information you feel you need to improve effectiveness in your role as a TA within the school, department/key stage, classroom team, or at the individual pupil level?	Systems that already exist	Ways to further develop active information sources
At the whole school level TAs need? e.g. an understanding of the school's management system; identification of which personnel to go to for specific support and direction; knowledge of the daily events of the school. Other:		
At the classroom level TAs need? e.g. an understanding of the long-term, medium-term and short-term curriculum planning, e.g. programmes of study for the year and the term, weekly/daily lesson planning.		

At key stage TAs need? e.g. to know which individual or small group they are working with for different lessons and an understanding of the lesson objectives.		
At department level TAs need? e.g. an understanding of where information can be read about the school as a whole, e.g. policies and the department or key stage e.g. resources, shared timetabled areas etc.		
At the individual pupil level TAs need? e.g. to understand the individual learning objectives for specific pupils they are working with and an awareness of changes to pupils' circumstances which may have an affect on their learning or behaviour.		
Other information I need to be effective would be:		

This form can be photocopied. © *A Toolkit for the Effective Teaching Assistant* 2004.

In discussion, TAs have teased out various examples of helpful 'active systems' These have included the importance of:

- school induction meetings for new staff;

- a short early morning meeting for all staff on a daily basis;

- the school prospectus, staff information board, teachers' planning on the school's intranet site;

- joint planning time built into contracts to review classroom planning or Individual Education Plans.

(b) Opportunities for discussion time between teachers and TAs

A key stressor mentioned by both teachers and teaching assistants is the **lack of time** to meet to discuss roles; pass information; share planning and evaluate educational process and progress.

Teaching assistants often express their concerns that teachers are so busy that they feel it is 'difficult to know when to try to speak to them'. Teachers on the other hand often feel that the only time they have available is before or after the pupils arrive or leave the classroom. This leaves them with a moral dilemma that: 'given a TA's pay and conditions, it does not seem appropriate to ask them to stay in their own time'.

In researching the views of teachers and TAs in relation to '**time to talk**', a balance of **informal** and **formal** times seemed to be used for different reasons.

Informal time, before or after lessons, or in the staff room, often focused on immediate lesson content, resources and individual pupil needs; these discussions were often spontaneous, acted upon immediately and generally went unrecorded.

Formal, scheduled discussion focused on joint planning and evaluation. These involved a much greater depth of communication and outcomes were recorded. Discussion not only centred on what strategies, approaches and resources were in use, but why and how all parties contributed to overall effectiveness and future developments. Significantly, it was also apparent that teachers and TAs felt that they listened more actively to each other during scheduled discussions, providing a platform for positive action. They remarked on a genuine feeling of creativity and collaboration, and a mutual empowerment within this positive work environment to maximize their own potential as well as that of their pupils and the school.

Activity

This activity provides an opportunity to audit the time currently spent by yourself and teachers in discussing work issues. It may help to pinpoint how and where those practices are efficient or could be developed.

The activity can be carried out by TAs, or teachers and TAs together.

When and why do you talk with your teacher/teachers?	What impact does your talk time have?	Is the amount of talk time appropriate for this issue? If not how could this be addressed?

A commonly expressed concern from TAs is the availability and access to the content and objectives of lessons. This often leads to a feeling of individual frustration over their own planning and lack of resource preparation and a feeling that their impact is ultimately less effective. Teachers who give TAs information about lesson content in advance and provide them with opportunities to participate in ideas and adaptation to tasks for specific children often feel that they are using the TA as a very real learning resource and TAs feel they have a specific and targeted role in the teaching and learning process.

Examples of HLTA Standards relevant to this theme are:

3.1.1 They contribute effectively to teachers' planning and preparation of lessons.

3.1.2 Working within a framework set by the teacher, they plan their role in lessons including how they will provide feedback to pupils and colleagues on pupils' learning.

Within the HLTA Standards (Appendix) there are other examples that relate to planning and expectations of teaching and learning activities.

Formal meeting times which are set up on a regular pattern need a clear purpose and format to ensure that the time is used efficiently. The inclusion in such meetings of time for immediate concerns tends to maintain a good equilibrium of short and long term issues. A brief record of the main points of the dialogue helps to maintain the focus and bridge the gap between meetings.

There also need to be simple, effective alternatives to meetings for some of the ongoing daily communication issues so that precious time is not wasted. This is particularly important and relevant where teachers job share; TAs move across the school; TAs are part-time, or supply teachers are utilized. Examples include: an agreed system of recording pupil needs; an appropriately located bulletin board with key, non-confidential information; and with many TAs having internet access at home, e-mail updates and contact.

It has been my finding that many TAs feel that they would prefer to meet and give up their own time than not to meet at all. They believe that this makes a significant contribution to job satisfaction. In response, schools can show their recognition of the time given by providing TAs some non-contact time within their working hours, or proposing some flexibility in contact hours, especially if the TA is studying for a qualification.

Clear scheduling and a guide to the intended content of whole school meetings with advanced publication provides opportunities for future planning.

Finally, both short, informal chat time and formal meeting times outside of the contact with children are essential components in communication networks. However, because of the complex nature of organizations and people, it should be borne in mind that these will rarely be perfect.

(c) An ethos of collaboration and inclusion in planning about pupil learning

Lacey (2001) considered differing levels of interaction, namely, **liaison, co-operation, co-ordination and collaboration**. She challenges our perceptions of teamwork by suggesting that:

> it is often argued that the word 'team' is used when 'work group' would more accurately describe the manner in which people are working together. They work alongside each other co-operating and even co-ordinating their work, but they are not a fully fledged collaborative team.

During sessions on teamwork teaching assistants from primary, secondary and special schools have been asked to consider the terms used by Lacey in relation to their working partnerships with teachers. They immediately recognize the four different levels and can identify the different interactions and provide examples. The following are indicative of their deliberations.

From experience, liaison often occurs in a corridor, or over a 'snatched' cup of tea and incorporates brief interchanges of information about pupils' learning or behaviour. Although a vital component of the total communication system, the content of the message should be carefully considered.

Co-operation can happen in respect of the introduction, or continuation, of a strategy or resource over an agreed period of time, even when team members have different opinions over the viability of the initiative.

Co-ordination appears to involve additional planning: for example, when dialogue and action takes place to reduce unnecessary overlap of resources or roles, so everyone knows their part in the strategy and when and where to carry it out.

Collaboration involves spending 'quality' time together for planning and evaluating the teaching and learning taking place in the classroom.

Tilstone, Lacey et al (2000) recognize that teachers and TAs have dilemmas about when and where TAs can take part in planning and state that:

> it is not right to expect them (TAs) to plan (especially as the lesson is in progress), produce resources, evaluate and record progress for the pupils they work with. Neither is it right for teachers to do all this for them without consulting, expecting them to carry out their plans without question. There needs to be a balance of the two.

The blurring of roles necessary to be collaborative is often difficult because of existing values, attitudes and beliefs about their own role, or those of their working partner. For example, both may hold the belief that teachers are in charge and should do all the planning without any TA involvement. Or both may believe that TAs are not able to give insights about children's learning which are relevant to planning. Both of these beliefs are underpinned by issues such as pay differentials; creating time to talk; a view of the professionalism of teachers and perhaps the self esteem of both teachers and TAs in relation to their working partnership.

However, importantly, Lacey (2001) suggests that teachers and TAs often recognize that the benefits of collaboration outweigh any of the practical and philosophical difficulties. Many teachers and TAs who work at developing collaborative practice would agree that the process and product can reduce stress. Empathy, creativity and productivity are all increased, resulting in a greater understanding of each other's skills, furthering professional development, and clarifying both collective and individual responsibilities.

The role of senior management should not be underestimated in the introduction and promotion of collaborative practice across the school: for example, the appointment of a senior teacher with responsiblity for ensuring that collaborative practice takes place and the introduction of references to collaboration in all job descriptions.

On the Foundation degree TAs have shared other ways in which their schools have encouraged an ethos of collaboration and helped to develop it in daily practice. Schools have used INSET days for joint teacher and TA training in collaborative ways of working. Others have audited the use of time across the school to identify places in the year, term, week, day and lesson where collaborative practice can be supported within school hours.

Activity

Teamwork processes

With a teaching colleague discuss how the processes of teamwork are used in your classroom context.

Give examples of where your partnership has involved:

- liaison

- co-operation

- co-ordination

- collaboration

Identify any difficulties for you and your teacher in maintaining, developing, or extending collaborative practice in your classroom or school.
How can you overcome those difficulties?

Difficulties with, or barriers to developing, extending, or maintaining collaborative practice	Ways of overcoming the difficulty and sources of support

This form can be photocopied. © *A Toolkit for the Effective Teaching Assistant* 2004.

(d) Recognition of the part TAs can play in 'differentiating' work for pupils

Differentiation has traditionally been part of the teacher role, and as Visser (1993) points out:

> it is not a new idea which emerged with the introduction of the National Curriculum but has been what teachers do, in that differentiation is the 'matching of teaching and learning styles'. The NNC (1993) defines differentiation as 'the matching of work to the abilities of individual children, so they are stretched, but still achieve success'.

He also emphasizes the need for differentiation for the individual to be set within a group teaching context and not to be seen just as individual work:

> the process whereby teachers meet the need for progress through the curriculum by selecting appropriate teaching methods to match an individual child's learning strategies, within a group situation.

The role of teaching assistants has developed and extended with TAs taking part in the teaching process and consequently differentiation has become a natural part of that role. Sharing differentiation can therefore either be an effective part of the teacher and TA partnership, or a source of difficulty depending upon the views held within the school, or by teachers and TAs.

First it is important to describe types of differentiation.

Differentiation of content:

- individual pupils can be taught in 'smaller steps' than their peers, so the curriculum framework is varied in its structure for some pupils;

- skills from an earlier key stage might be reinforced within the context of a higher level programme of study with careful selection of content and age appropriate resources and approach;

- pupils follow the same topic but study and develop certain aspects in more depth;

- different resources may be used to achieve the same learning objective.

Differentiation of task:

- a range of different activities;

- activities linked to the pupil's interests;

- recording the activity in a different way e.g. scribing.

Differentiation of learning outcome:

- learning outcomes could be differentiated in relation to different performance criteria e.g. use of 'P' scales in key stage assessments etc.

Differentiation of level of support:

- more individual time given to a pupil by the teacher or teaching assistant;

- pupil groupings can be arranged to be supportive and varied;

- more support given to preparation and reduced one-to-one support to enable pupil independence.

Differentiation in teaching style:

- a wide range of teaching approaches can be used to suit a wide range of learning styles e.g. visual approach, VAK = visual, auditory and kinaesthetic, multi sensory etc;

- flexibility of approach;

- adjust the speed of the work task;

- adjust the speed of the programme of study;

- provide repetition of concept;

- pupils work at different rates on the same tasks, so the pace is varied to suit individual needs.

Differentiation of resources:

- use additional resources, special aids, or modified resources to support learning;

- use strategies to make curriculum materials relevant, clear, interesting and achievable.

TAs may have little knowledge of the modes of differentiation and can benefit from discussing the techniques and considering when to employ them and with which pupils. TAs could also possibly benefit from more professional development in this area. The desire to maximize pupil potential is difficult to realize when faced with a lack of strategies and understanding, but especially when there is an expectation that you will be able to support individual pupils with special educational needs.

A knowledge of positive intervention strategies which can be used flexibily as a situation demands is recognized as a part of 'good teaching' and no matter how well prepared a teacher or TA is for a lesson the interaction of the pupil with the material often still demands varying degrees of differentiation depth.

TAs do this in many different ways and these are often very effective and for the purpose of this chapter and activity the phrase 'on the spot differentiation' has been used.

An example of an HLTA Standard relevant to this theme is:

> **2.3   They understand the aims, content, teaching strategies and intended outcomes for the lessons in which they are involved, and understand the place of these in the related teaching programme.**

Within the HLTA Standards (Appendix) there are other examples that relate to the knowledge and understanding of TAs.

Activity

On the spot!

Make a list of your own 'on the spot strategies' in relation to enabling pupils to successfully carry out their school work.

Compare these thoughts with other TAs and teachers in your school.

Photocopy the activity below and consider the general strategies that both TAs and teachers can use in situations where children require individualized support to enable them to be successful in their learning.

Evaluate your own use of these strategies and also compile a bank of strategies for your own use and that of colleagues.

'On the spot' strategy	General example	Own example
Simplifying the language used to describe the task or activity	'Where the worksheet says . . . we are going to find out . . .'	
Explaining words that the child does not understand.	Encouraging the older or more able pupil to use a dictionary to search for extra information.	
Focusing the pupil on one or two aspects of a worksheet or task only.	'You are going to work on questions 1 and 3 first.'	
Writing, to highlight key parts of a task, activity or worksheet to enable the pupil to see clearly what they are aiming at doing.	Use a highlighter pen to underline key words or the questions to focus on.	

Using drawing to highlight key parts of a task or worksheet.	Pupil to illustrate the answer by drawing/tracing/copying.	
Helping the child to organize his/her thoughts to consider how to set out the task.	Using a prepared set of symbols to order the task for a pupil who requires this level of symbol support rather than just written. Have a written sequence list.	
Using concrete materials to illustrate a task or concept.	Use 3D or 2D materials.	
Using a pupil's own interest area to illustrate a concept.	If child likes soccer explain the number concept in terms of a football team etc.	
Giving the pupil a choice of aspects of the task or worksheet to be concentrated on and then spending more time on those aspects.	'We could do this worksheet this way . . . or this way . . . what do you think?'	
Using a tape recorder to record ideas or a computer to record the information.	Record suggested answers on the tape recorder. Transcribe answers by writing or wordprocessing as appropriate. Use the internet to research information. Use software relevant to this topic.	
Other strategies used in your work context		

This form can be photocopied. © *A Toolkit for the Effective Teaching Assistant* 2004.

Discussion between teachers and TAs about these strategies can mean more effective opportunities for successful pupil learning.

Sometimes these roles are carried out by TAs or by teachers but without discussion. If they are made an overt part of the partnership, this can deepen reflection on practice, and practice itself. It could, for example, lead to IEP targets stating the differentiation that would potentially demonstrate more variation in levels of pupil progress.

It is also important that where possible pupils understand the differentiation levels which help them be effective learners. For as Visser (1993) says 'differentiation must aid pupils to become independent learners'.

(e) Communications between teacher and TA to develop a shared perspective on understanding pupil needs

Sometimes, teachers and teaching assistants do not share a common outlook on children's needs as a result of differences in their personalities, life experiences, beliefs and values.

This can make the partnership less successful, but there are occasions when differences can occur in any working relationship and these differences need not mean that the partnership cannot work.

Katzenbach and Smith (1993) cited in Lacey (1998) even suggest that teams or partners who work beyond the natural comfort zones of constant agreement on issues may be able to develop greater success in their working relationships:

> real teams can be identified by the ability of their members to take risks, to use conflict positively, to trust each other and to work interdependently, using mutual accountability to evaluate their practice.

Activity

Three way communication

The following practical exercise focuses on a scenario that most teachers and TAs have experienced to some extent in their day-to-day practice in the classroom. It is also a scenario in which teachers require support and feedback to enable them to develop their differentiation levels.

Read the following scenario.

You have been asked by a teacher to do a piece of work with a pupil who has special educational needs. The worksheet is not at a level to keep the pupil's attention and cannot be completed easily by the pupil without further adjustment.

Photocopy the activity and consider what you could do to:

- make the breakdown in communication between teacher, pupil and TA worse;

- differentiate and enable the pupil to learn;

- communicate with the teacher about this situation to provide a long term approach to differentiation for this pupil.

Discuss this scenario with your teacher and consider how the teacher would prefer such a situation to be handled.

How could you make the breakdown in communication between teacher, pupil and TA worse?	
What could you do on the spot to differentiate and enable the pupil to learn?	
How could you communicate with the teacher about this situation to provide a long-term approach to differentiation?	

I have asked TAs to discuss this scenario and to consider where or how they can make this situation better or worse and the frustrations involved for all parties. TAs often suggest that:

- An immediate, outspoken, negative comment about the handout would imply a criticism of the teacher and make the pupil feel inadequate.

- The issue of TAs not engaging in any alternative strategies and just 'doing what I am told' can slowly make the situation worse for all three participants.

- TAs could make use of some parts of the worksheet or adapt it by using some of the strategies identified in the 'on the spot' activity, to enable immediate access to learning.

- Breaking the task down and giving genuine, appropriate encouragement and incentives or rewards could be a good way of establishing a positive outcome for the pupil.

Further discussion of the dilemma involved, often establishes that feedback to the teacher is an essential component of the TA role. However, communicating concerns in the right way is something that can prove difficult and TAs often agonize over what to say and when to say it.

What is clear from above is that some attitudes, values and practices need to be addressed.

In this process of consideration TAs need to think about concentrating their communications on what **the pupil was enabled to do** rather than an over emphasis on what the **worksheet did not provide**.

Showing the teacher the pupil's finished worksheet can illustrate the pupil's level of access to the work and be a useful starting point for a discussion on what the pupil managed to achieve from the exercise and then what the pupil found difficult.

Sometimes time prevents this level of immediate discussion and so a positive, written comment is an alternative way of communicating the learning that took place and how it was supported.

Describing to the teacher what was done to enable the pupil to take part can lead on to discussions on some of the ways that the teacher would like worksheets or activities differentiated and the information feedback given in the future so that a clear system emerges.

On many occasions, both teachers and TAs speak of the ways in which they avoid any open disagreements and feel that this will maintain harmony, e.g.:

I say nothing even when I disagree, I just get on with the job.

However when teachers and TAs reflect on their communication levels they realize that their body language, tone of voice, etc. are all part of the communication and these may have given a very different message than the words used.

A consideration of possible reactions could fall into three categories, namely: non-assertive or passive-aggressive; aggressive, or assertive.

The examples given below are gleaned from TAs own experiences.

Non-assertive or **passive-aggressive** reactions to potential strategies and approaches could be:

- disinterested or dismissive facial responses e.g. raising eyebrows;

- body language e.g. folding arms and turning slightly away;

- remaining quiet, or no vocal response e.g. silent or muttering a reply.

Aggressive reactions to potential strategies and approaches could be:

- negative comments e.g. 'it will never work, we have already tried that kind of thing before and where did it get us then?'

- negative actions e.g. placing equipment down forcibly on the table.

Assertive reactions when there are new ideas or there are issues not resolved could be:

- communicating that it is good to consider the issue: 'I think it is good that we think this through.'

- communicating what your initial feeling to the strategy or idea is: 'I feel on first hearing this that . . .'

Activity

Consider the way you interact within your classroom partnership when you are considering new strategies with a pupil; or you have to make changes in the classroom.

Evaluate the responses in relation to the examples of non-assertive reactions, aggressive reactions, and assertive reactions given above.

Another potential challenge may be that TAs want to ask for greater involvement in the classroom planning and workings of the class. Many teachers welcome this and recognize the benefits of sharing some of these roles rather than feeling isolated. However sometimes TAs do not know how to accomplish this or they ask in a way which implies criticism of their teacher colleague.

It is important the TAs and teachers understand the need to have assertive communication that is built upon genuineness, empathy and respect for each other's roles.

Assertive communication involves describing how you feel, a description of the effect of an action or behaviour and a request for what the person would like to happen. Therefore a comment from a TA which says:

> I feel worried when we do not have time to discuss next week's planning because I want to support you and the children as effectively as I can.

remains assertively focused within the TA and teacher relationship and roles. Both teachers and TAs need time for training in supportive teamwork practises as these are often the key to success within classrooms.

Activity

Establishing a shared perspective.

Sometimes the teacher and TA partnership can break down and then can be hard to re-establish.

What can teachers and TAs do when they cannot find a shared perspective from which to move forward in planning for pupils' learning?

Consider what factors enable a teacher and TA to develop a shared starting point for communication.

What recording systems are already being used in the classrooms you work in for establishing good communication about pupil needs and developing a shared perspective?

CASE STUDY EXAMPLE

During a school outreach setting I experienced a teacher and teaching assistant who were not speaking a great deal to each other due to a disagreement over the way a pupil with attention deficit and hyperactivity disorder (ADHD) was being taught and supported in his classroom.

After consulting with the teacher the latter expressed her view that the pupil was being over protected by the TA who, she said, allowed the child far too much time and attention instead of being more directive with the pupil and insisting on boundaries. The teacher felt that the pupil was manipulating this TA.

The teaching assistant meanwhile reported to me that the teacher did not understand the pupil and would never give him any time to focus in the lesson and that if allowed a little 'off-task time' the pupil would gradually accept redirection without getting angry.

Both staff showed their notes on the child's participation in lessons over the last week in relation to his on-task behavior.

One showed the pupil having had a less than satisfactory week with some lessons in which he was very disruptive; whilst the other showed that the pupil had had some good parts to the week.

It was difficult to get a real picture and the notes though carefully kept were written from the perspective taken by the teacher or the perspective taken by the teaching assistant and measured within their own perspectives.

Drawing on my impartial status as a visitor to the school, we got together around a table and discussed the issues. Subsequently, together they devised a joint recording system which involved a simple scoring system from 1–5 with clear criteria for each score recorded in relation to specifically targeted behaviours.

Working with other teaching assistants

TAs need to establish positive working practices between each other. Without such collaboration some pupils may not experience the continuity of provision and learning support that they are entitled to. TAs can often provide each other with a very useful source of professional development provided they are given time to collaborate.

In some schools there may be more than one TA working in a classroom or several in one department and therefore the management of each of the staff member's roles and responsibilities can become even more complex with even more collaboration required.

Some of the ways of encouraging reflection on the variety of TA roles within the school, and an understanding of the similarities and differences of various TA roles, can provide valuable evaluative insights, and possibly decrease misunderstandings between TAs carrying out very different responsibilities but all within the wide brief of the TA role. Schools can encourage an ethos of:

■ Sharing and interchanging roles. For example, a TA who is one-to-one with a pupil and a TA who is considered to provide general classroom support. They may have more understanding of each other's roles if they interchange on an agreed and organized pattern, after consultation between the TAs and the teacher.

■ Observing the roles played by TAs in other classes or departments, or with specific pupils to provide a broader understanding of the needs of the school, the staff, the pupils and the curriculum.

■ Sharing care roles with academic support roles. A rota or rolling system organized to ensure that these roles are shared can ensure that TAs feel valued and treated equally.

■ Induction and professional development. Where one TA is an established staff member and another TA is new to the class or department, an induction period to review the expectations of the teacher and the class or lesson routines and to develop confidence may need to be set up and discussed by all the team members. The role of the established TA may also need adjustments in light of new staff and these issues need to be a clear part of any class or team meetings.

An example of an HLTA Standard relevant to this theme is:

> **3.3.6** They are able, where relevant, to guide the work of other adults supporting teaching and learning in the classroom.

Within the HLTA Standards (Appendix) there are other examples that relate to supporting teaching and learning.

Working with pupils in small groups

As TAs take on more and more small group work with pupils through initiatives such as Additional Literacy Strategy (ALS) and Springboard Maths, it is important that they receive training in how groups form and develop so as to have appropriate analytical tools to reflect on their own performance as group manager and facilitator.

An example of an HLTA Standard relevant to this theme is:

> **3.3.5** They advance pupils' learning in a range of classroom settings, including working with individuals, small groups and whole classes where the assigned teacher is not present.

Within the HLTA Standards (Appendix) there are other examples that relate to supporting teaching and learning.

Tuckman (1965) provides five key stages of development that 'groups' go through.

■ **Forming.** Group or team members are establishing their **rapport, relationships and roles.**

■ **Storming.** Group or team members are establishing their **differences** in rapport, relationships and roles.

■ **Norming.** Group or team members are **settling into a pattern** of rapport, relationships and roles.

■ **Performing.** Group or team members are **working at their optimum** within their established rapport, relationship and roles.

■ **Mourning.** Group or team members are going to be leaving their group setting and experiencing change and are **evaluating** their rapport, relationships and roles.

Such knowledge and awareness can also be applied to the teamwork process and TAs should recognize that working partnerships can go through developmental sequences.

Activity

Small groups are teams too.

Considering the groups of pupils with whom you work, can you give specific examples of behaviour which show that the group has transferred through, or is going through, the stages outlined by Tuckman?

If our goal is 'performing' then how can you encourage small groups of pupils to move through the sequence?

Tuckman stage	Observations of group behaviour/actions/attitudes	Strategy for group progression
Forming		
Storming		
Norming		
Performing		
Mourning		

This form can be photocopied. © *A Toolkit for the Effective Teaching Assistant* 2004.

Summary

In the busy life of the classroom reflecting on our partnership roles can seem less important than other more pressing issues. However reflecting on teamwork issues can be vital if the relationship between teachers and TAs is to be positive and their roles to be complementary in the teaching and learning process.

This chapter has suggested that the supportive partnership between a teacher and a teaching assistant needs to have:

- an understanding of each other's roles and responsibilities;

- respect for each other's strengths and weaknesses;

- willingness to use objective criteria for analysing class issues or pupil difficulties;

- an understanding of how personal some issues can feel and a willingness to de-personalize for the benefit of pupils, e.g. their behaviour;

- the capacity for telling each other what has gone well and congratulating positives on a regular basis;

- setting problematic feedback about difficulties with pupils within a generally positive working framework.

In order to develop the levels of good communication necessary for positive teamwork teachers and TAs need to feel that they have the confidence to reflect openly on their own practice and that of their colleagues. Teachers and TAs need a level of self esteem which allows them to reflect openly on their skills and the way these interrelate in a teamwork setting.

The next chapter discusses the way that self esteem affects our thinking and actions and how self esteem can be a vital part of our personal and professional development of practice.

Further reading

Balshaw, M. (1999) *Help in the Classroom*. London: David Fulton.

Lacey, P. (2001) *Support Partnerships. Collaboration in Action*. London: David Fulton.

Tilstone, C., Lacey, P., Porter, J. and Robinson, C. (2000) *Pupils with Learning Difficulties in Mainstream School*. London: David Fulton.

Self Esteem – Enhancing the Role of the Teaching Assistant

This chapter will consider the following key themes:

- understanding the importance of self-esteem;

- links to learning;

- emotional literacy;

- strategies for positive behaviour management;

- the self esteem of the teaching assistant (TA).

Understanding the importance of self esteem

The aim of this chapter is to explore issues relating to self esteem, not only that of pupils, but also for you as a TA and an educator. As adults working in schools, we are all educators, whatever our title or role. Each interaction we have as a member of staff is critical.

Through our responses to each other, we are subconsciously setting the climate for relationships within the school and also modelling this to pupils. This is a critical concept. A positive learning environment can only occur if all feel valued, have a voice and are heard.

How might the following pages prove useful to you?

You may read this chapter on one occasion when you are focusing on a child you know well and feel has low self esteem. In your search for answers you will be looking to try to understand their needs and also strategies to support and develop self esteem.

The first half of the chapter focuses on this aspect with interwoven case studies of pupils. An example of an HLTA Standard relevant to this theme is:

> **1.2 They build and maintain successful relationships with pupils, treat them consistently, with respect and consideration, and are concerned for their development as learners.**

On another occasion, however, the focus of your reading may be your role and your attempts to gain a greater insight into your own personal and professional development and practice.

Responses from research conducted with TAs have been included to illustrate this.

An example of an HLTA Standard relevant to this theme is:

> **1.6 They are able to improve their own practice, including through observation, evaluation and discussion with colleagues.**

Activity

How well do I support and relate to the pupils I work with?

How do my professional relationships make me feel about myself and my role?

What are the indicators that let me know that I am valued?

Who are the people important to me within my role?

The responses to the questions above will enable you to begin to consider which aspect of self esteem you wish to focus on in the first instance.

It is important that we as educators provide structure and opportunity for young people to reflect on who they are, and to be confident within themselves and with others as they learn and mature through each interaction, whether in a formal structured teaching environment or informal contact in corridors and the playground. Understanding the system, policies and practices within your workplace and supporting them can help you in this task.

A positive and motivated school as described in Chapter 1 provides such a system. We must also recognize that a school, like any complex organization, will face challenges and will not always provide a positive environment for all pupils and staff.

Therefore, rather than focus solely on the notion of either low or high self esteem I would like you to consider the notion of **self esteem as a continuum**.

With this perspective, our main aim could be to enable a child to move along that continuum, increasing their self esteem from low towards higher. We must bear in mind that the journey along the continuum may take some time and indeed for some, may never be achieved within the school setting.

It may be that in your role you only have the opportunity to work with a child for a short period and not see the outcome of your work. How we, as educators, manage our interactions with pupils is critical if we are to begin to create and reinforce a positive sense of self. It is vital therefore to focus on what we can do. If we can enable a positive change, no matter how slight, we begin to enhance the development of self concept and a sense of self linked to successful learning and social experiences.

There are many opportunities to encourage the development of a positive sense of self esteem within the school setting. Teaching assistants are in an ideal position to address this in terms of their role through their involvement with pupils, teachers and the curriculum and their active support of agreed school policies and strategies.

Developing an understanding of the importance of self esteem and how it links to both achievement and the development and sustainment of positive relationships is crucial.

A school offers the opportunity for us to use a systematic and structured approach, yet allows roles to be sensitive and respond to the needs of individuals, pupils and staff.

The nature of the role you have, and the opportunity to develop supportive relationships with pupils, also enables you to become alert to their sense of self esteem, and their perception of how successful they are at learning new tasks and acquiring new skills, enabling you to plan your approach to meet each individual's needs.

Becoming aware of the fragility of self esteem in some pupils is the first stage in identifying an opportunity to begin to intervene and thus start to enable the pupil to have the confidence to begin to grow and develop in their sense of self.

As educators, I believe we need to be aware of the degree of responsibility we have in our interactions with others, be it adults or pupils. Whilst it may be that it is unlikely that we will be able to change the behaviour of others (unless they choose to do so), we can endeavour to ensure that when we leave an interaction none of those involved feel worse for their contact with us. A TA is often the link between teacher, pupil and in some situations parents, thus is at the heart of developing and sustaining positive relationships, ensuring pupils are able and willing to engage with the learning process.

An example of an HLTA Standard relevant to this theme is:

1.5 They are able to liaise sensitively and effectively with parents and carers, recognizing their roles in pupil's learning.

What do you understand the term self esteem to mean?

Activity

What does the term 'self esteem' mean to you?

Can you define it?

Previous definitions have included:

> Self esteem arises from the discrepancy between the perceived self, or self concept (an objective view of the self) and the ideal self (what the person values, or wants to be like). A large discrepancy results in low self esteem, while a small discrepancy is usually indicative of high self esteem.
>
> (Pope et al., 1988, p. 4)

> Self esteem is the individual's evaluation of the discrepancy between self-image and ideal self. It is an affective process and is a measure of the extent to which the individual cares about this discrepancy.
>
> (Lawrence, 1996, p. 5)

> Self esteem is the respect and value of the self. It is the concept that there is real importance in what we do, think, feel, and believe.
>
> (White, in Bovair et al., 1993, p. 100)

> Self esteem is the ability to see oneself as capable and competent, loving, unique and valuable.
>
> (Berne and Savary, 1981, p. xiv)

For me the essence of self esteem is defined as a sense of:

- competence;

- being valued;

- being loved.

If these are the crucial elements of understanding self esteem, you may like to consider these elements both in terms of a pupil(s) you support and your role.

Activity

Identify specific times when you felt:

- valued;

- acknowledged for your individual commitment and competence at a task or activity.

What did others do or say to give you this feeling?

Reconsider your own earlier definition of self esteem. Is there anything you would add?

As you read the activities in this chapter maintain your new definition at the forefront of your thinking.

How do you believe pupils would respond if you asked them the same questions?

Activity

Consider how a child assessed as having low self esteem may present in your class or school.

How would they:

■ behave?

■ respond to a task or an instruction?

■ relate to others?

■ respond to change or new situations?

Consider the following case studies.

CASE STUDY EXAMPLES

Harry is 15 and has a Statement of Special Educational Needs. He is described by staff as frustrated and often directs his anger at peers and staff. He will refuse to undertake work which he considers beneath him, but at times gives up when work is set for the whole class that he feels that he cannot complete, yet he is reluctant to accept help.

He has an older sibling who is often in trouble. Staff recognize the surname and sometimes assume they have a troublemaker in class, confusing him with his sibling. His behaviour has been described as inconsistent – one day he is pleasant, cheerful and works well, responding positively to encouragement, another day he is rude, disruptive and apparently lazy.

Amber has a Statement of Special Educational Needs for Specific Learning Difficulties (SpLD) and is described as healthy looking and well dressed. She is of average height and build and is described as a quiet, shy and thoughtful child with a kind and caring nature. She is openly friendly with all her classmates yet finds it difficult to form close friendships amongst her peers and so often seems lonely. In the classroom she hides behind her long hair, especially when asked difficult questions. She will avoid tasks at times and can talk out of turn. Attendance is a concern as she has frequent absences from school.

These pupils are different, in age, gender and most specifically their individual needs. Yet to staff they represent two pupils who are not only having a negative experience of school and the process of learning but could both be described as having low self esteem.

Is it possible, therefore, to support the development of a positive sense of self esteem when pupils have such different needs? I believe it is.

Understanding the sense of self

The starting point for an understanding of the pupil's sense of self is the careful consideration of the potential reasons behind their actions or responses.

Harry and Amber, plus other pupils, may believe all or some of the following statements:

- I find it difficult to relate to others, so begin to believe that no one likes me and I have no friends;

- no one values me;

- I cannot learn and I am stupid;

- I find many tasks in school 'high risk' (e.g. learning new skills, completing tasks) and avoid them in whatever way I can;

- I am afraid of allowing myself to begin to form attachments or connections with pupils or getting involved in situations that would allow me to grow and develop as a person;

- I often feel anxious and seek to please others;

- I have strong feelings, but am often either scared of expressing them or unable to manage them;

- I don't think much about myself and reinforce my negative perception of myself by making self-disparaging comments – I'm thick!

It is clear, therefore, that pupils with low self esteem do not feel:

- **Capable** – that they are able to complete tasks. Harry and Amber either avoid tasks by rejecting them or by their behaviour.

- **Lovable** – that they are unique as a person. Harry is often mistaken by staff for his older sibling who is disruptive, and may not feel recognized for himself and what he can offer.

- **Valued** – that they can contribute. Amber, whilst friendly with her classmates, is unsure of her place in the group and what she can offer thus tending to isolate herself.

Pope, McHale and Whitehead (1988) consider self esteem in children in five areas:

- **social** – how they feel about themselves and others;

- **academic** – the child's evaluation of themselves as a student;

78

- **family** – his/her sense of place and belonging in the family;

- **body image** – physical appearance combined with capabilities;

- **global** – a general appraisal of the self.

If we apply this model to Harry and Amber, then I would consider social and academic areas as those in which they may need some support. Harry may also feel that the reputation of his sibling influences others opinions about him and thus he may feel that his sense of place within the family has an impact on the school setting.

Jim (below) is also affected by this, but his sense of place within the family is in relation to a change in his family setting.

CASE STUDY

Jim is in Year 1. He was 'chatty' last term (summer), but at times is now sullen. He lacks confidence when faced with new tasks and seeks reassurance from his teacher and TA. They describe his behaviour as attention seeking with low-level behaviour difficulties and deduce that he is a 'bright child, but lazy'.

At times he interferes with others' work and makes sure staff know that others have made errors in their work.

Staff have observed that there are tensions developing in his friendships.

A new baby was born in the summer holidays.

Amber, Harry and Jim may appear to behave or act in ways that would indicate that they have low self esteem, but still try, often with great success, to mask their feelings about:

- competence at the task;

- relationship with others;

- or their place within the group.

Activity

Consider the pupils in your class.

Do they hide behind a mask to avoid a task or new activity that may involve risk or potential failure, e.g. 'class clown', 'Mr/Miss Helpful?'

What are these 'masks' that the pupils you know put on?

Jim is Mr Critical, he may feel that other pupils aren't doing things properly and if he can point this out, he can show that he is not the only one to get things wrong. If he can highlight others' shortcomings he can avoid criticism of his efforts. Very young children are often unsure about their sense of self and try different masks to find out 'Who am I?', 'What am I like?' In this example staff in school felt this was not the case and that he was responding to the change in his home circumstances.

When Amber is asked a question that she does not understand or want to answer she becomes 'Miss Invisible' hiding behind her hair hoping not to be noticed. Contrast that with the attention she draws to herself by talking out of turn, 'Ms Notice-Me'.

Harry at times is 'Mr Superior – this work is beneath me', and at times 'Mr Angry', probably in classrooms where the staff have confused his identity with that of his sibling. He feels angry that they have not noticed him for himself and knows that his sibling presents challenging behaviour in class, so concludes that he might as well act up to the mask he's been given.

The table below summarizes the elements that makeup the elements of self esteem. They are interrelated and each contributes to the growth of the other.

Competence	Being valued	Being loved
Learn new skills	Have a sense of self	Relates to a significant other
Practise skills	Accept recognition of success	Recognizes feelings
Achieve competence	Reciprocate recognition of success with others	Accepts relationships
Have the confidence to try new activities	Have a sense of their own identity and role in relation to the group they belong to	Knows they are loved

Figure 4.1 further demonstrates the flexibility and creativity we need when supporting the development of self esteem and indicates how as a TA you have the opportunity to begin to intervene to build, even though it may be in small stages, a positive sense of self esteem in pupils. For each pupil the point where you can connect and intervene may be different, but as the model below indicates, wherever you enter, it is the beginning of developing a sound sense of self and positive self esteem. I believe for all we can begin to connect through one of these three elements.

We can reverse the arrows or interject at any point in the cycle.

It is not about failing to achieve it is about the response to the failure. We need to teach pupils that we learn through failure and that it is OK to fail as that is how we learn and that we need to take risks to do so. If we are confident to take risks we will learn and begin to build confidence and thus begin to feel more competent.

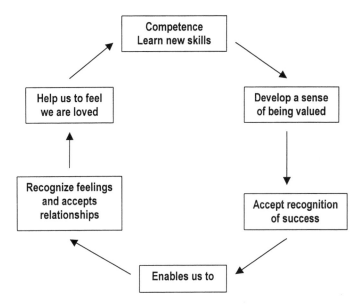

Fig. 4.1 Stages for building self-esteem.

Activity

How do you respond when a young person you work with fails to achieve at a task or activity?

Do they receive the message that you expected them to fail or do they feel ready to learn from the experience and try again?

Reflect on your findings. Your responses to pupils when they are not successful at tasks is critical. The focus must be on ensuring that the pupil feels confident in tackling the task; a relationship based on mutual respect and trust will enable this to occur. Although some pupils may resist support after they are unsuccessful at a task, you need to ensure that the quality of the relationship is maintained and be sensitive in the way in which you approach this. If a pupil does not feel competent, this will affect how valued and lovable they feel. Remember that how we feel about ourselves may make a difference to the way in which we work with pupils and there will be times when we need to acknowledge our emotions, for if we too feel that in our role as educators we lack competence, are not valued or recognized for who we are and what we can contribute, we will not be effective in our role. We must ensure that we are still able to effectively support the learning of the pupils we support.

What is self esteem?

Lawrence (1996) constructed a model that considered self esteem as an embracing term for specific elements in the study of self.

Self image and **ideal self** which combine to give us:
our **self concept**.

Self esteem, therefore, can broadly be defined as the inner picture we hold of ourselves.

Self image

This could be considered to be *what the person thinks of themself*. Lawrence (1996, p. 3) describes it as:

> . . . the individual's awareness of his/her mental and physical characteristics.

This will have begun to be formed in our earliest days, within the family and our social contacts.

Consider a baby's surprise when biting their toes for the first time, a sensation that lets them know that these feet are a part of them. It is the start of an awareness of body image which grows and changes as we get older; meet and mix with others; influence and are influenced by others. This awareness continues and aids the development of our self image as we begin to decide who we are; perceive a sense of how loved we are; or what abilities we have or do not have.

These perceptions are strongly influenced by both verbal and non-verbal messages we are given as we grow and mature. Consequently, it is vital that we recognize the importance of the **quality of the interpersonal relationships** we develop and the demand for **high level of communication skills** when working with pupils.

Your role as a TA can determine the quality of relationships for a pupil as some will need more structure and nurture in their interactions with other adults within the school setting. For example, pupils with an existing low self image will readily accept and internalize a casual negative remark that will reinforce their existing poor self image.

Your role may need you to alert other adults either teaching or supporting the pupil to be aware of the need to choose language carefully when either correcting behaviour or explaining a task or activity.

As children enter puberty and adolescence body image often becomes a high priority. The importance of how they perceive they look, or trying to be part of a group, or part of a 'look' can be the source of much anxiety and stress.

By understanding the importance of the elements of self image as part of self esteem, we can be more aware of the difficulties for some pupils despite the positive strategies implemented in school.

Broadly speaking these elements will include consideration of our:

- physical appearance – what we look like;

- skills – what we can/cannot do;

- how we relate to others – the ability to maintain and develop relationships;

- how we manage ourselves and our emotions.

All of these combine to build our self image. Harry, Jim and Amber all have difficulty relating to others and managing their emotions. Whilst Jim and Harry are more demonstrative in their emotions, Amber is quiet and withdrawn. All indicate they have problems in maintaining and developing relationships with their peers. In some circumstances they indicate a lack of confidence in skills for a task and, as a result, either do not attempt it or sabotage their own success.

An example of an HLTA Standard relevant to this theme is:

3.3.3 They promote and support the inclusion of all pupils in the learning activites in which they are involved.

Ideal self

This is a consideration of what the person would like to be – their 'ideal'. Over a period of time it may take into account the messages received from other diverse sources. This includes the individual's collected experiences and who they want to be, their own goals, aspirations, expectations and dreams, but with the added complication of considering what they think other people think of them. Clearly, this is a difficult aspect of self esteem for some pupils.

Confusion can arise as we process information from many different sources. How we analyze and act on this information and what part of our ideal self the information relates to will all be taken into consideration. At different times there may be more sensitivity to the development of our ideal self within home, school, or social or other highly influential settings – the influence of what parents, carers, other influential adults and significant peers think. Inner conflict may be created for the individual because of the influences of these different groups.

Pupils may feel that at times they are striving for an image that is unattainable.

Jim finds it less threatening to criticize others rather than acknowledge their skills and success.

Harry tries to be positive on some days, but is overwhelmed by a negative sense of self and so gives up.

Amber is unsure, on the outskirts of the group.

A greater sense of self may enable them all to join in more confidently and acknowledge recognition for themselves.

Self concept

Our self concept is our perception of who we are, our own identity. This links in with our personal map of all our relationships both in our personal lives and in our roles as educators, our understanding of the people around us, our personalities and our individual responses to situations. It is made up of three elements:

■ how we think and connect thoughts – cognitive;

■ how we feel and respond – affective;

■ what we do and how we behave.

Harry, Amber and Jim have all been supported by TAs who believed in them and who used strategies that enabled them to begin to develop a more positive sense of self concept.

Why is it difficult to change self concept?

As **self concept is a personal evaluation**, based on our individual interpretation of events, experiences and interactions, it is difficult for another to intervene, even when it is clear to those around us that we are sustaining and reinforcing a negative image of ourselves.

Harry's self concept is determined by what he thinks teachers and his TA think of him. If he feels they do not really know him as a person and value him for himself, but only have 'their perception' of him (which might also be confused with a sibling), then he sees no reason to change. His negative sense of self concept is being reinforced by those around him.

Lawrence (1996) considered this aspect of self esteem theory in the context of his research and identified four characteristics of self concept. You may recognize these from the pupils you considered in a previous task.

Characteristics of self concept (Lawrence 1996)	Some basic points to consider
Avoidance Quiet, shy, may be withdrawn. Will avoid the situation that may expose failure.	Do they appear upright in their posture, using eye contact where appropriate? Do they join in with activities? Are they part of a group? Does the pupil participate or avoid involvement in a task or activity?
Compensation Outgoing, dominant personality. May fight back rather than risk failure.	Do they question either the relevance of activity or their involvement in it? Do they move from group to group? Do they appear to fall out frequently with others? Are they fearful of being put down, tending to criticize first?
Motivation Negative perception of the self illustrated through comments, remarks made.	Do they repeat the same task or activities and appear to fail deliberately? Do they start and restart a task? Do they initiate activities or wait for individual instruction or guidance?
Resistance Rejects any support or guidance offered.	Do they reject any support or guidance even when they have not understood the focus of the task or activity? Do they avoid adult approval during task completion?

(Adapted from Lawrence, 1966)

Activity

Reflect

Using the model above consider what strategies you would you use for Harry, Amber and Jim.

In his early writings (1968) Abraham Maslow identified a hierarchy of needs, within his theory a prominent position was given to self esteem. Maslow proposed that in order to achieve 'potential' and learn, we must have our needs met as we pass through a series of stages.

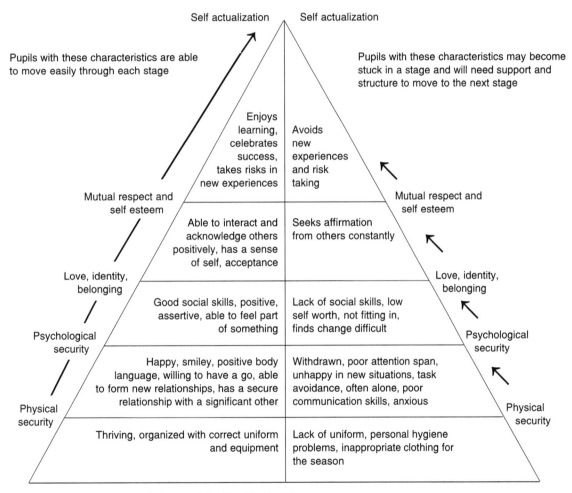

Maslow's hierarchy of needs: pupil characteristics identified by TAs

Training materials developed for the implementation of the Behaviour and Attendance strand of the Key Stage Three Strategy (DfES, 2004) also make this link and emphasize the importance of understanding Maslow's stages in promoting effective learning opportunities. It is important to recognize that a structured response to positive behaviour management within a school promotes **behaviour for learning**.

As you can see from the diagram above a positive response to pupils who are 'stuck' within a level is crucial if their needs are to be met and an opportunity to reach self actualization (in this context learning) is to occur.

Clearly links can be made to the Inclusion, Behaviour and other policies within your school at each stage of this model and reinforces aspects of self esteem that we have already examined.

Activity

Do I recognize these stages of development?

Assess if you support these stages within your school setting.

Identify what you do now and what you need to do to ensure that you actively support these stages.

Identify the links to the school behaviour policy.

An example of an HLTA Standard relevant to this theme is:

3.3.4 Teaching and Learning Activities use behaviour management strategies in line with the school's policy and procedures.

I have also used Maslow's model to consider the role that a TA could have in supporting systems and structures within school settings and to consider the needs of individual pupils, by building sensitively stage by stage. Conclusions reached after discussions with TAs are summarized in the table below.

Maslow stage	TA strategy
Self actualization	Affirm as a person, recognize and acknowledge success
Mutual respect and self esteem	Praise and encouragement, respond to individual needs, give time

Love, identity and belonging	Express an interest in the pupil, acknowledge strengths and interests, be a good listener, acknowledge and affirm, use positive non-verbal signals, use reward system
Pyschological	Acknowledgement of the person, positively reinforce task or behaviour, allow time for interactions between TA and pupil, check pupil's understanding of task or events that have happened, collaborate with teacher over differentiation, use behaviour policy to structure interaction
Physical	Greet each pupil by name, smile, use school interventions to address physical needs e.g. spare PE kit

Developing emotional literacy

Much has been written recently about **emotional intelligence** and **emotional literacy** and how a greater understanding of these concepts can enable us to be more effective in our roles in supporting the teaching and learning experiences of our pupils.

Whilst some imply that the terms are interchangeable, I prefer to view them separately and in this context focus on the process of understanding and managing emotions.

The links between understanding and managing emotions and the development of self esteem are critical in ensuring the optimum environment is created for learning to be both meaningful and successful for the pupil and educator involved.

Salovey (1989) defines emotional intelligence as:

> The ability to monitor one's own and other's feelings and emotions, to discriminate among them and to use this information to guide one's thinking and actions.

Goleman (1996) defines emotions as:

> *not* just intangible but chemical and neurological responses essential for survival and well being.

and notes that:

> . . . IQ at best contributes 20% to factors that determine life success.

The opportunity exists therefore for educators in schools to ensure that their influence, through the relationships they develop, is positive. We should consider the impact we can have in providing the right kind of experiences not only for successful completion of tasks and achievement of potential, but for consolidation and transference of success to other settings and experiences.

Whilst this clearly links to self esteem, it also indicates the degree of self awareness that is necessary, particularly for you as a TA, in the role you have with individual pupils in creating the opportunity for learning to take place. Responding appropriately to the emotional needs of pupils and ensuring these needs are met requires skill, sensitivity and empathy.

An example of an HLTA Standard relevant to this theme is:

2.5   They know the key factors that can affect the way pupils learn.

Harry's TA had to plan carefully as his responses to either the task set, the teacher, or other pupils were so varied and unpredictable. She had to be aware of her own behaviour and how she responded when he was particularly challenging.

Understanding your own emotional responses in the context of the needs of individual pupils will enable you to contribute directly to a classroom climate that openly supports the needs of all learners for both educators (adults) and pupils. Hay McBer (2000) identified that 'a positive classroom climate includes feeling emotionally supported, empowering pupils to try new things and learn from mistakes'.

Activity

What are my beliefs about emotions and learning?

What is my classroom climate? (Chapter 1)

What do I contribute now?

What changes could we discuss? (Chapter 2)

How might this impact on teamwork? (Chapter 3)

Do we need to consider:

structures that are in place;

implementation of policies – the interpretation of policies in the classroom;

relationships;

acknowledging individuals;

learning activities?

An example of an HLTA Standard relevant to this theme is:

2.9   They know a range of strategies to establish a purposeful learning environment and to promote good behaviour.

What can we do?

You can teach pupils to understand and express emotional needs clearly and also provide positive feedback to pupils and colleagues.

As a TA you need to demonstrate how to connect **positive actions** that support an individual pupil's recognition of a sense of self or identity and thus support their development of a sound self-concept (through, for example 'self talk', see below).

You can also (where appropriate) share personal emotional responses demonstrating the skills of empathy and understanding.

Strategies for positive behaviour management

In order to begin to manage behaviour effectively we need to understand ourselves and how we react when dealing with behaviour difficulties. This knowledge enables us to begin to be aware of the powerful influence that we have over how a young person feels.

The table below outlines some strategies that can build self esteem and promote positive behaviour management.

Strategy	Example	TA
Positive statements	The use of a positive record book or diary.	Amber's TA used this to enable her to record success and reflect on her feelings with weekly sessions to discuss this. Jim's TA used a daily positive statement book and stickers.
You and I messages	Modelling positive language by using I statements, encouraging activities e.g. circle time that use I statements: I am worried, I feel happy.	Harry responded well to modelling using positive language. Jim's TA actively adapted her language to I messages.

Strategy	Example	TA
Positive self talk Teach children positive self talk and ways to overcome and bounce off some of the negative messages directed back at them.	Allow pupils to visualize scenarios in which previously they have been unsuccessful, provide them with positive statements to overcome their perceived sense of failure and offer ways of achieving real success. Talk them through a different approach to a problem. This is a systematic strategy that works.	Harry needed a 'script' for lessons he found challenging particularly the first ten minutes when he found it hard to settle. Amber responded to metaphor e.g a curtain coming down for not understanding a task, staircase for success.
Affirmations These build on the power of self talk and can be used in many ways.	I am valued in my group. I belong to this class. My skills are valued.	Amber and her TA used daily affirmations. Jim's TA used them to reinforce one-to-one sessions.
Recognition	Can be unconditional (for the person) or linked to tasks. Both must be meaningful and affirming.	TA communicates to teacher. Harry, Amber and Jim's TA all ensured this happened and used smiles, stickers, certificates, comments.

An HLTA Standard relevant to this theme is:

3.3.2 They communicate effectively and sensitively with pupils to support their learning.

We, as educators, are part of the process of developing self esteem in pupils. Consider the potential negative influences that we can present.

- Emphasis on negative language to describe events with no recognition of what has gone well. For example, a noisy lesson with a group, ignoring the quality of the task and completion that may also have happened.

- Using assemblies and other times when pupils are in large groups to repeatedly stress situations that may only apply to a few e.g. uniform infringements, litter, movement around the school.

Often there are **pressure moments** within a school timetable when staff responses to these stressors can culminate, often accidently, in what Canfield and Wells (1976) called '**killer statements**'. These manifest themselves as either verbal or non-verbal negative statements that can have the effect of making someone feel worse as a result of an interaction. They undermine an element of an individual's self esteem. They may be in the way we speak, not only to pupils, but also to colleagues, the words we choose, or the emphasis, tone of voice, or accompanying gestures.

Activity

Be honest – what killer statements do you use?

Are you more likely to use verbal or non verbal behaviour?

Are there some times of the day or week when you are more likely to use more killer statements?

We must be aware that pupils acutely observe our interactions and, therefore, opportunities exist for modelling clear communication and positive interaction with our colleagues. The quality of relationships we have with the other adults we work with will determine the effectiveness of the learning environment for the pupils.

An HLTA Standard relevant to this theme is:

> **1.4 They work collaboratively with colleagues, and carry out their roles effectively knowing when to seek help and advice.**

> I have come to a frightening conclusion. I am the decisive element in the classroom. It is my personal approach that creates the climate. It is my daily mood that makes the weather. As a teacher I possess tremendous power to make a child's life miserable or joyous. I can be a tool of torture or an instrument of inspiration. I can humiliate or humour, hurt or heal. In all situations it is my response that decides whether a crisis will be escalated or de-escalated and a child humanized or de-humanized.
>
> (Hiam Ginott, 1972)

The language, both verbal and non-verbal, that you use, not only to pupils but about them to other adults in the school setting, can influence the development of the young person's self concept. Skills of communication are vital in underpinning the relationship that exists between staff and pupils. These skills may need to be taught to the pupils, but first consider yourself.

Activity

Ask colleagues to observe you as you interact with pupils and record the context (as you may find that your responses change in different situations). Consider:

What body language do you adopt?

What words do you choose to use?

Do your words and gestures match?

How do you communicate with the teacher or other adult in the situation?

How do you use space and move around the classroom?

What is the first strategy you adopt in addressing a behaviour problem?

What are the outcomes?

Did you 'escalate' any situation?

An HLTA Standard relevant to this theme is:

3.1.2   Working within a framwork set by the teacher, they plan their role in lessons including how they will provide feedback to pupils and colleagues on pupil's learning and behaviour.

CASE STUDY EXAMPLE

Cleo is studying on our Foundation degree. As she has been a TA in a primary school for a number of years she decided to take the opportunity to focus on her behaviour and responses from pupils for an assignment. She was confident that she could demonstrate how her beliefs about a positive approach to behaviour management enhanced her pupils' learning opportunities. Rather than rely solely on feedback from colleagues who observed her she arranged to be videoed, in order that she could analyze it herself. Cleo thought that she was always positive in her interactions with staff and pupils. She always thought about her choice of language and chose her words carefully. However, she was not prepared for what the video revealed. She did use positive language, but when the sound was turned down it revealed that her non-verbal language was much more powerful than her verbal language and was not empowering and affirming, but critical and at times judgmental. This enabled Cleo to understand why she did not always get the response from pupils that she wanted. Other staff in the school also chose to be videoed and analyzed their own behavior. The outcomes surprised them and contributed to the professional development of all involved.

Cleo's experience may enable you to understand why you are not getting the response you planned for. Rogers (2000) refers to the notion of congruence: the words you use and the way in which you deliver them should match. Disparity in either will block communication with the pupil you are supporting. These are skills that need to be recognized and practised (Chapter 3). Completing a task such as the one above can also improve communication and collaboration between staff and enable you to provide evidence to meet HLTA Standards, for example in this case Standard 1.6.

The self esteem of the TA

Research with TAs beginning their studies on the Foundation degree elicited the following responses.

Words to describe me as I am now: self image	How I would like to be: ideal self
Uneasy	Confident
Lacking in confidence	Self assured
Out of touch	Outward going
Tired	Not stuttering
Agitated	Calm
Preoccupied	Happy
Apprehensive	Relaxed
Curious	Even tempered
Excited	Self assured
Tense	Liked
Interested	Tactful

These comments all relate to the self esteem of the TA, and therefore will affect how the TA is able to work alongside the teacher to support effective teaching and learning in the classroom.

Activity

Reflect

Do you identify with any of the comments in the self image column?

What can you do to overcome some of the negative feelings and identify with the more assertive comments in the second column?

Do you need more information from colleagues, for example, or to clarify your role in a specific situation?

The **Johari Window** is a model we can apply to looking at self and encourage us to look at our sense of self with regard to our professional role. It was designed by two psychologists, Joseph Luft and Harry Ingham (cited in White, 1995).

The use of a window as 'an analogy of a model of self' is apt as it allows us to hide as much, or reveal as much, as we choose.

It is apposite in considering the role of the TA as your professional role is evolving and changing not only in response to your individual needs but in the wider context of change within schools and the remodelled workforce (Chapter 2).

Briefly the model is as follows.

	Known to self	**Not known to self**
Known to others	**Open** What I know about me and what you know about me. You can see this all the time. TA responses: I know I am flexible, reliable, consistent, fair, informed.	**Blind** What I do not know but you can see about me. If you share this with me and I acknowledge it, this information will be in my open window. TA responses: others can see I have high expectations and reflect on my practice.
Not known to others	**Hidden** What I know about me and what you do not know. I keep this hidden, I may share it with you and if I do this information will then be in my open window as we both know.	**Unknown** What I do not know about myself and you do not know about me. I can only find out through new experiences and taking risks where I feel safe. I may keep it hidden from you, you may see new skills

TA responses: others cannot see my apprehension, hiding emotions.	and attributes and not tell me so I am blind to them or I may find things out and share them in my open window. TA responses: finding I can do things I never thought I would e.g. being confident when talking to teachers.

TAs on our Foundation degree completed this by focusing on their perception of the role of a TA. Examples of their comments are included above and indicate how the role of the TA changes as confidence increases and acknowledgement from others occurs.

Activity Johari Window

Complete your own Johari window
Consider how this highlights your strengths and skills
Can you match any of these to HLTA Standards highlighted in this chapter?

	Known to self	Not known to self
Known to others	Open	Blind
Not known to others	Hidden	Unknown

Summary

Understanding the importance of the role that you have within a learning organisation is the beginning of a process that will hopefully enable you to develop a clear sense of purpose. Without that it will be more difficult for you to promote self esteem as part of your practice. The language you use, your non-verbal communication and the types of interactions you display to other adults in the school give an indication of the degree to which you are committed to ensuring that relationships and communication are valued and acknowledged. Pupils will be aware of the quality of relationships they observe.

Acknowledge yourself and all your positive qualities and successes every day !

Further reading

Greenhaigh, P. (1994) *Emotional Growth and Learning.* London: Routledge Falmer.

Lawrence, D. (1996) *Enhancing Self Esteem in the Classroom.* London: Paul Chapman Publishing.

Long, R. and Fogell,J. (1999) 'Self esteem' in *Supporting Pupils with Emotional and Behavioural Difficulties.* London: David Fulton.

Supporting Learning and Teaching

This chapter looks at ideas about how children think and learn and the way they are taught and will consider the following:

- getting to know the learners;

- 'surface' learning and 'deep' learning;

- Piaget's idea of schemas, assimilation, accommodation and equilibration;

- learning styles: reflector, theorist, pragmatist and activist styles, VAK;

- Vygotsky's ideas of collaborative learning and ZPD;

- didactic and collaborative styles of teaching and learning;

Why do some learners fail to succeed?

When reflecting on ways in which to become most effective in supporting learning and our own teaching, it is often helpful to be able to relate our thoughts on these areas to particular individuals and their learning problems.

For example, let's take 'Albert' who appears to be lacking in success at school.

Do the problems lie internally with Albert, for example his inability to concentrate, his perceived laziness, his lack of motivation, his intelligence or is it just being a boy?

Or are they promoted by external factors: for example being dropped on his head as a child; lack of stimulation at home or poor parental support, perhaps he watches too much TV?

Or is lack of success caused within the environment of the school?

Nature v nurture

The big question might be is it to do with his 'nature' (genes) or the nurturing process he received at home, in his social life with his peers and friends, and at school? This of course is the classical debate of nature v nurture which so often gets constructed in terms of people being determined by one or other of these factors. I feel it would be much more fruitful if we considered the influence of both.

Aspects of nurture

In this chapter, the nurturing process which we are most interested in is that of how Albert's teachers and teaching assistants (TAs) might influence him and his learning within the school environment.

Amongst the possible in-school 'roadblocks' to learning could be:

- the lack of an infectious, enthusiastic teaching environment, even boring classes;

- a lack of organization or clarity in the presentation of work which in turn confuses Albert;

- a feeling of being alienated by the culture;

- individual learning needs are not taken into account and, as a result, appropriately differentiated, stimulating resources are not provided.

These are pretty big questions and they might all be in play at some time for Albert. As TAs you are employed to be part of a team that helps to maximize the potential of each pupil and to make them feel valued as individuals.

Can we help Albert?

A good first step would be to grab his attention. We have to remember that we need to engage him as an individual learner and to try to encourage his involvement with the other learners in the group. Teachers and TAs do this through the use of high order, interpersonal skills, actively seeking to encourage Albert to offer something about himself, possibly a positive event in his day, or a strongly-held personal interest. On this they build the foundations of a relationship and then tackle his assessed academic needs. This identifies a key principle in effective practice that we **teach people first**.

How can we help him?

If we get this order of events right we have a better chance of responding more positively alongside pupils like Albert. This means 'feeling the emotional temperature' of the classroom situation.

Activity

Getting to know your learners

How do you get to know a new group of learners?

What exercises do you use?

Do you have some really effective methods which have been successful?

What are you trying to achieve by doing this?

Consider the following statement: 'we teach people first and subjects as a secondary activity'.

Does your evaluation of this statement influence your thinking and practice?

Getting to know and relate to our learners is essential, but within the classroom setting helping them to become more effective learners is our central task. Of course we hope that our concern for them as individuals will motivate them to want to achieve higher levels of learning and thus become more confident within the school setting.

As part of this 'press for achievement' in a good school (Chapter 1) the TA has to consider the important structures of the learning process and how these impact on the individual learner. Just as in Maslow's Hierarchy of Needs (1970, Chapter 4), learning is most likely to be successful if certain basic conditions are met and the foundations are laid towards 'self actualization'. However, if insufficient attention is paid to assessment, planning, preparation, delivery and evaluation to meet the needs of the individual learner, then, if learning takes place at all, it is likely to be at what Marton et al. (1984) described as '**surface**' learning.

The 'depth of learning'

At this level:

> The student reduces what is to be learned to the status of unconnected facts to be memorized. The task is (merely) to reproduce the subject matter at a later date, e.g. in an exam.
>
> (Gibbs, 1992, p. 2)

Many writers have considered the composition of learning and the impact that such ideas may have on what makes a successful learner. A main aim of education must be to move all learners, including ourselves, from operating at 'surface' level to a much '**deeper**' level. This might be categorized as being attained when:

The student attempts to make sense of what is to be learned, which consists of ideas and concepts. This involves thinking, seeking integration between components and between tasks and playing with ideas.

(Gibbs, 1992, p. 2)

Activity

Moving from surface to deep learning

Think of a time when you felt really comfortable in a learning situation and as a consequence you learnt something at a deep level.

What part do you think the teacher/trainer had in this process?

What were the emotional qualities in this process?

When considering the idea of surface and deep learning we are of course considering different levels of thinking. Bloom (1956) presented a hierarchy, classification or taxonomy (see table below). As you move down the table the 'engagement with deeper learning' intensifies.

Competence	Potentially demonstrated by	In the classroom, demonstrated by
Knowledge	Recognition of recall of information Knowledge of dates, events, places Knowledge of major ideas.	Lists, description, labels, who, when, where, etc.
Comprehension	Understand information Grasp meaning Translate knowledge into new context Interpret facts Compare and contrast.	Summarize, contrast, predict, associate, estimate, discuss, extend, etc.
Application	Use information Use methods, concepts, theories in a situation different from original learning context.	Apply, demonstrate, calculate, complete, illustrate, show, solve, modify, relate, change, experiment, discover, etc.

Competence	Potentially demonstrated by	In the classroom, demonstrated by
Analysis	Seeing patterns Organization of parts Recognition of hidden meaning Identification of components.	Separate, order, explain, connect, classify, arrange, divide, compare, explain, infer, etc.
Synthesis	Uses old ideas to create new ones Generalize from given facts Relate knowledge from several areas Predict, draw conclusions.	Combine, integrate, modify, rearrange, substitute, plan, create, design, invent, what if? compose, formulate, rewrite, etc.
Evaluation	Compare and discriminate between ideas Assess value of theories, presentations Make choices based on reasoned argument Verify value of evidence.	Assess, decide, rank, grade, test, measure, recommend, convince, select, judge, explain, discriminate, support, conclude, compare, summarize, etc.

(Adapted from Bloom, 1956, cited on website www.coun.uvic.ca/learn/program/hndouts/bloom.html).

However, even in the most stimulating of educational settings, it does not necessarily follow that deep, or even deeper than surface, learning will occur. Sotto quotes Polyani, (1994, p. 54) with regard to some of the factors that are involved in 'trying' to learn.

For deep learning to potentially occur there is still a requirement that over the learning period other **essential contributors** are present. For example:

- discovery – that in the learning process there will be 'something' that we do not know – but the acquisition of this 'something' would be beneficial and we 'need to know' it;

- immersion in the problem;

- puzzlement – the journey will not be simple, there will be 'challenges' and at times uncertainty;

- active engagement, especially in obtaining information and testing hunches;

- repeated exposure to the learning situation;

101

- the presence of an 'expert' who can set up a situation, act as a model of competence, answer questions;

- periodic insights into the direction of learning and possible outcomes;

- feeling of pleasure from gaining these insights;

- doubt that one will ever really understand and a faith that one will finally understand.

Already we have established that creating the environment and opportunities to maximize learning is complex. All of these ideas are important for your attempts to move your learners towards deeper levels of learning, and encourage 'lifelong learning'. To try to create optimum conditions for learning you will need, amongst other skills, knowledge and understanding, the capacity to examine how you recognize and develop empowering relationships and how you, yourself can demonstrate your own 'deep learning' by analyzing, synthesizing and evaluating some of the strategies you use to enhance pupil motivation and successful learning engagement.

Ideas about learning

Piaget (1896–1980) was one of the most influential writers on the ways in which we learn. I believe that he would have agreed with many of these ideas especially that of being actively engaged in learning through new experiences.

How would Piaget begin to explain how Albert feels about being at school?

Like us all, Albert's head is full of ideas, thoughts and memories from his past and indeed aspirations for the future. These are ideas he has accumulated through his experiences both about himself and of his world and which he has internalized and made his own. This is a process Piaget called **assimilation**.

Albert builds up a range of thought patterns (or schemas) which guide, and even sometimes control, his behaviour. They could be likened to scripts or prompts which we read in order to remind us about the world and which also help us know what we can expect of it and how we can predict its behaviour. These schemas are very necessary in the process of accumulating our understanding of our world but, equally, can prove problematic if they become fixed and unchanging.

In new situations, Piaget suggested, we need to change them through a process of what he called **accommodation**.

For example, when Albert finds himself at his new, large secondary school for the first time he might have to change some of his ideas (the existing schemas in his head). In his comparatively small primary he had been used to being the first in the queue for lunch. However, today he is in a different environment, but still with the same schemas and scripts about the world and therefore the same expectations. In this new environment there are many more people who also want their lunch at the same time as him. He quickly finds that getting what he wants is more problematic.

102

Now Albert, and possibly many of the others who may also not have learnt the art of waiting and sharing, has at least two choices here. Through some rather quick learning he could **assimilate** the new environment and its conditions, **accommodate** these with his existing schemas, adapt and change his behaviour and wait his turn. Alternatively he can leave his existing schemas intact without any accommodation. In this case he will soon find that the world is rather less accommodating and that at some time he will have to learn to change his behaviour or live with the pain of having to fight the world single-handedly, a potentially painful process, but one which we know many children go through.

Activity

Trying to change our schemas and our behaviour

Can you think of a time when you, as a TA, did or did not, change your ideas (your schemas) about a new working environment that you were in?

Can you remember the outcomes of that piece of thinking and possible behaviour?

How might these ideas relate to, and explain, the behaviour of some of your learners?

As a biologist, Piaget had observed plants and animals needing to achieve a level of homeostasis (a need to maintain the same state of being) usually with regard to keeping warm and having enough nutrition and water. This physiological state of balance is also necessary for human beings but is equally necessary in terms of their thinking and feeling about the world, their **psychological state**. Piaget came to believe that there has to be accommodation because most people feel most uncomfortable when 'out of balance with the world'. Piaget called this equilibration. If this is so then Albert needs to balance his original schema about always getting his lunch first with the reality of his new environment and the equally demanding presence of others. He requires a more equal balance between his thoughts and his new world; he needs to learn a new set of schemas.

These reflections on changing thinking lead on to one of the most important issues educators have to recognize – that in the learning process, there is a great deal of **unlearning** to do if we are to accept new ideas about the world.

Unlearning some of our most cherished ideas and concepts about ourselves and our world is often quite difficult. Many of these ideas come to us either through our direct observations about the world or through being told by others of their 'truths'. Thus we gain a store of common sense, or at least sense which is commonly held by many others.

Alternative ideas

Over the years there has not always been agreement about the definition of learning, especially in educational circles. Woolhouse suggests:

> Learning occurs whenever a person adopts new, or modifies existing patterns of behaviour in a way which has some influence on future performance or attitudes.

> (Woolhouse, et al., 2001, p. 12)

This process is possibly something like the concept described by Kolb (1983) in his Cycle of Experiential Learning which starts with real experiences and, through a reflexive, thinking process leads to new learning (see Fig. 5.1).

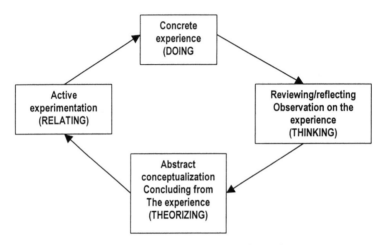

Fig. 5.1 Adapted from Kolb (1984).

Is this how we see Albert changing his view of his new school environment where he starts with a new concrete experience of the world, 'having to wait for his lunch', then reflecting on the situation, thinking about what it means for him and then deciding what to do about it?

If he changes his behaviour we can assume that some new learning has taken place and that he has adopted some new ideas or modified them, thus changing his old schemas.

Certainly that's what we hope, and schools expect, he will do to get back to a state of balance in terms of his thoughts and behaviour in regard to his new experience at school.

We can see from this model the need to provide real, concrete experiences, but in order to learn from them we need to promote reflection on our values, attitudes, beliefs and behaviour and consider how this affects us and other people.

These ideas fit quite well with Honey and Mumford's (1986) notions of the possible ways in which people learn through **doing, thinking, theorizing and relating to the real world in a pragmatic manner**. They suggest that we all experience these four learning processes, though not necessarily in the order suggested in Figure 5.1, nor with equal intensity, or to equal levels.

If, after a lesson, we ask pupils how they have learnt we often get some interesting responses:

> I like to have a go and see what happens even if it goes wrong and I wanted to ask lots of questions about it before anyone else did.
>
> (Activist)

> I like to gather information and mull things over. I was trying to work out what it has to do with what I already know about the subject.
>
> (Reflector)

> I like to tidy up and reach some conclusions. I asked questions to see how these new ideas fitted with my own ideas. Also I was trying to work out if I could think of a logical way of solving the problem posed in the session.
>
> (Theorist)

> I like tried and tested techniques that are relevant to my problem.
>
> (Pragmatist)

Honey and Mumford's concern is to observe how people learn within this 'framework'. We all use 'theories' to help us understand our world and so that we might also be 'reflective' about our actions. In addition we often need to know how things 'work in practice' and may often just need to jump in and 'have a go' at things often on a trial and error basis without too much thought. There may however be one or more of these elements which are dominant and our preferred style(s) in our approach to learning and some style(s) in which we are less comfortable and in which we may need to become more adept.

We all know about people who act before thinking and who may also not reflect on the consequences of their behaviour or its affect on others. Conversely some people do too much thinking and reflection and this may mean that they never try things out in practice or may never volunteer knowledge in a whole class setting.

Work on learning styles offers guidance on how we prefer to learn and is an important part of our toolkit in assessing how our pupils are engaging in learning. If, for example, you as teacher have a preferred learning style and always approach your teaching from this perspective, then there is a possibility that your teaching may not be engaging with potentially 75% of the group of pupils who do not share this style.

They will also have quickly detected this one-dimensional approach and potentially lost motivation to be part of the learning experience.

Activity

Consider the figure below. Can you identify some preferred learning styles amongst your pupils?

If so are you potentially teaching to their perceived strengths?

PRAGMATIST The learner might demonstrate this preferred style through being: ordered; structured; practical; accurate; organized; hands on; detailed; exact
they may learn the best through: checklists; outlines; charts; summaries; data; use of laboratories; use of computers; practical reading; short lectures

---

REFLECTOR The learner might demonstrate this preferred style through being: sensitive; emotional; imaginative; colourful; deep feelings; flexible
they may learn best through: group discussion; media and music; peer group work; role play; use of fantasy and imagination; themes; arts; humour; short lectures

---

ACTIVIST The learner might demonstrate this preferred style through being: independent; creative; risk-taking; inventive; problem solving; curious; investigative; intuitive
they may learn the best through: games and simulations; problem solving; creating products; independent study; experiments; opportunity to demonstrate unusual solutions; options; open-ended work; few restrictions

---

THEORIST The learner might demonstrate this preferred style through being: logical; academic; structured; intellectual; a reader; researcher; evaluative; thinker; debater; studious
they may learn the best through: reading; lecture; working alone; term papers; library work; note-taking; essays; research

---

So, as a simplistic example, if your own preferred learning style is Activist and you make this your main teaching style, then you will probably be keen to promote independent study and offer opportunities for pupils to learn with few restrictions. However if a quarter of your group are Reflectors, who essentially prefer humour imagination and engagement, then they might find the whole experience frustrating and pointless.

Peter Honey's Learning Styles Questionnaire is, quite correctly, protected by copyright. However, when offered the chance to complete it people quickly recognize themselves and their preferred learning style. Should you wish to investigate this further refer to Peter Honey's website. (NB: the learning skills questionnaire can be completed on-line for a fee at www.peterhoney.co.uk.)

Complementary to preferred learning styles is the concept of preferred methods of receiving and perceiving information. This recognizes the fact that we take in information via a range of senses:

■ visually through our eyes;

■ through auditory stimuli;

■ kinaesthetically, through our sense of touch, by feel and physically engaging with the world. This is encapsulated in the familiar VAK (visual, auditory and kinaesthetic) ideas about learning styles or preferences.

Research suggests (Smith, 1998) we prefer to learn predominately through a specific stimulus. So, **visual learners** will 'see' concepts in their minds and be able to recall them more readily. For them graphs, charts, posters, keywords displayed and mapped out will help their learning. Also they may tend to talk in visual images, 'I see what you mean'; 'I can't quite picture it'.

Those for whom an **auditory** stimulus is important will enjoy the engagement of discussion, hearing stories and will prefer to receive instructions verbally. They might be relied upon to remember verbal classroom direction given out by the teacher more readily than non-auditory learners.

Kinaesthetic learners may prefer to learn through doing and will certainly benefit from physical activity and concrete reinforcers. For them bodily movements, dance, PE and gestures are important when recalling events and describing ideas and concepts.

So, to try to maximize potential we need to ensure where possible that all senses are stimulated.

Activity

Keeping our learners 'engaged'

How do you ensure that your learners are 'engaged' through as many of their senses as possible within a classroom session?

What have been your most successful strategies?

What strategies do you know about but have yet to try out for yourself?

Learning and management of effective teaching is, therefore, clearly not straightforward. It should be noted that recently, Coffield et al. (2004) have questioned the assessment and value of learning styles. Their findings can be accessed at the Learning and Skills Research Centre at www.lsrc.ac.uk. Not only does it appear that people have differing preferred learning styles, we also know that children's and young people's understanding of their world is often quite different from that of adults. Depending on their age, they do not have the same range of contexts in which to set new ideas and thus very often misunderstand what they hear from adults. Their 'commonsense' understanding of the world is often quite different from ours and we know this sometimes to our cost, and especially if we do attempt to get into their 'field of knowing'.

An example is that of the movement of the sun in relation to the earth. Clearly, by every day observation we can see that the sun circles the earth. It is usually only by the 'authority' of others that we come first to accept, and then possibly later to understand, that the reverse is true. Even in the face of Galileo's evidence the Pope could not accept this truth and was thus unlikely to ever begin to understand it.

Some adults are like that about new ideas, but for children the problem might be different, they may not be ready, in terms of cognitive development, to accept such abstract ideas and thus not be able to explain how they happen.

Activity

Checking for understanding

Ask some of your learners about their understanding of some scientific concept.

For instance, how do clouds form? Where does water go when a wet piece of paper dries? Why does it get dark at night? Why do some heavy things float and some light things sink?

In response to these questions ask them how they came to know some of these things, who told them and when did they learn them?

An example of an HLTA Standard relevant to this theme is:

> 2.5 They know the key factors that can affect the way pupils learn.

Within the HLTA Standards (Appendix) there are other examples that relate to teaching and learning.

For Lev Vygotsky (1896–1934) the place of the teacher and initiator of knowledge was central in this learning process. The process of **joint learning** – pairing the more 'knowledgeable' with the less 'knowledgeable' – and placing the 'teacher' at the centre of helping children understand themselves and their world both as an educational and social process was essential.

He suggested that gaining and making personal sense of new knowledge was a two-level process. First, at an **interpersonal level**, between people and then, later, **intrapersonal** as the new idea or concept is internalized.

This process is one of mixing new ideas with an existing understanding of the world.

Since these ideas come partly from our personal understanding of the world and partly from other people's new ideas and we actively construct them for ourselves, rather then passively accept them, they are of course very personal 'constructs'.

Activity

Seeing the world from others' points of view

Can you recall a time when you were exposed to a new concept and managed to misunderstand it because you saw it from your own egocentric view point?

(The example that springs to mind for me is that of Laurie Lee's first day at school when the teacher told him to, 'sit there for the present'. On his return home his mother asked him how he got on. 'Oh, it was quite good, but I never got the present.' The teacher had clearly not de-centred thus not seeing the idea of present from the point of view of a child.)

Can you think of a similar example from your experience of working as a TA with young children?

This process of internalizing new ideas can be problematic since all of our individual understanding of the world will tend to differ to some extent. This is particularly the case where ideas about people's behaviour, values and cultural norms are concerned. In this process of aiding understanding of new ideas it is important to know what the learner already knows.

Vygotsky anticipated this process by suggesting that we can help people to move to another, 'deeper' level, or 'zone' of knowledge through what he called the **Zone of Proximal Development (ZPD)**.

Activity

Helping our learners to check what they already know

How do you attempt to find out what your learners already know, and possibly understand, when you are offering them some new knowledge?

This process of moving children to a new zone of knowledge and understanding starts by assessing what the child already knows. From there it attempts to build new knowledge on top of that existing knowledge and as near to it (in close proximity) as possible. In this way, the child is taken on to a new zone of knowledge which is commensurate with their ability to gain and understand new ideas.

This newly aquired knowledge and understanding will be different for each child, not only because their starting point of knowledge will be different, but also individual learning capacity at any one moment will be different for many reasons.

Helping children to connect with knowledge they already have is an appropriate way to commence teaching, but also a way of helping them to integrate existing knowledge with new knowledge thus deepening their understanding of new ideas.

So for Vygotsky the idea of **joint learning**, with the more 'advanced or accomplished' learner helping the less knowledgeable person to a new zone of learning, was central to the whole process of the acquisition of knowledge and its understanding. This process could be facilitated by an adult or a more knowledgeable pupil and offers an ideal of mixed ability teaching. In such a situation anyone could be both a teacher and learner with the teaching child moving possibly from 'simply knowing about a new idea' to 'understanding it' merely because s/he has articulated their ideas to someone else.

As teachers ourselves we know that often the best way to learn and understand new ideas is to teach them to others. Vygotsky offered us the rationale for doing this. He also suggested that this was positive socially, as it has the essential hallmarks of **collaborative learning** as opposed to a competitive striving for new knowledge.

Activity

Promoting collaborative learning

In what situations do you think it might be appropriate to encourage children to help each other to learn new ideas?

Do you have examples of where you have seen or practised such an approach?

What have been the benefits and/or problems?

Essential to this idea of collaborative learning for Vygotsky was that of the place and value of language. First, using language so that communication is at the child's level of understanding and second exposing the learner to richer and more complex language and thus developing deeper cognitive thoughts. For Vygotsky it is language, in its broadest sense that is the essential component in this cognitive process.

Since language is so important in the learning process it is essential that we use it carefully in our teaching, for example asking appropriate questions in order for pupils to make connections with their existing knowledge and to move them to deeper levels of understanding. Also we need to develop a dialogue with our learners so that they can articulate their ideas and thus understand them, and themselves, better. Socrates, over 2,400 years ago, recognized that learning was a two-way process and that rather than lecturing people it was better to enter into a dialogue. This approach also recognizes that people may know more than they think they do and that through an even-handed discussion there could be a 'journey of discovery,' not only of new ideas but of existing knowledge as well.

By asking the right questions at an appropriate learning level and listening carefully to the responses Socrates taught his untutored slave about trigonometry.

Activity

Consider the last day of professional development you attended.

Recall one new thing you learned on that day. (Product of session.)

How did you learn? (Process of learning.)

Thoughtful, sensitive responding is useful in terms of connecting and reassuring people about their own practice, the value of any learning experience and their self esteem. For example, a group of TAs when asked how they had internalized the main points from a session on how they taught the Additional Literacy Strategy (ALS) gave the following responses:

> Considering, asking questions, usually with a follow-up question, to see how their ideas fit with mine.
>
> (Theorist)

> Having a feeling of empathy with others helps me to recall and thus learn. For example, when there was a general misunderstanding about a feature of the ALS programme it made me think if I was fully aware of all the implications of that point.
>
> (Reflector)

> Matching what I got from others with my own knowledge helped and finding out how they operate in their own practice confirmed some of my ideas.
>
> (Pragmatist)

> Just getting in there and asking questions, not waiting for others to come to me.
>
> (Activist)

I have linked these responses to learning styles (see Honey and Mumford above) to illustrate the 'circular' nature of transmitting knowledge, and that there is often a connection with the way in which we engage with new knowledge and thus possibly remember it.

Impact on teaching

Reflecting on our own learning and our learning styles might suggest specific areas of strength and weakness and that there could be scope for improvement in our teaching styles, methods and approaches. We should be striving, to the best of our ability, to maximize the learning of all pupils by constantly examining our own teaching. When it comes to the issue of teaching style you should be very knowledgeable since, as teaching assistants, you have observed more teaching and teaching styles than most people. Only one group of people have seen more and that is your learners, the young people in your classrooms who sit day by day being exposed to many different teachers and their teaching methods and styles.

Activity

How to apply these ideas to your own class and your own teaching

Having thought about your learning style, do you actually teach in the way that you would prefer to learn?

Does this mean that particular pupils relate better than others to you?

What are their learning styles?

Do some pupils have more difficulty with the work you set?

To examine some possible teaching approaches and styles let's start with your experiences and ask you to recall both early and more recent experiences of teaching from the point of view of you as learners.

Activity

Remembering some significant learning moments

Recall your experiences of being taught:

1   As a child in a primary school setting (5–11)

2   As a young adolescent in secondary school (11–16)

3   As a post-16 student either at a sixth form or FE college (16–18) or as a professional (16–60).

112

Consider the style of teaching and its human approach and also how you felt in those different settings.

What emotions did you have then and now recall?

A traditional concept of pedagogy (teaching of children) suggests that learners were quite passive in the learning process likened to empty 'mugs' to be filled from the full 'jugs' of knowledge by their teachers.

Alternatively, other schools of thought suggest that there is a greater recognition of people's prior experience and knowledge and a concern to use that knowledge within the learning situation and to promote a more collaborative learning environment.

In this way they are engaging learners in three essential learning roles:

- they are the 'learner' receiving information;

- they are also a 'supporter' helping others in the group, and

- they themselves are a teacher/facilitator offering ideas to others.

In this second model there is a more even-handed sharing of knowledge and a more democratic level of power between teacher and pupil/student, both in terms of teaching styles and knowledge ownership. In addition the line between teacher and learner, which was often well defined in the pedagogic model, is less clearly drawn or needed.

In your work with your pupils/students you will use an eclectic mix of models of teaching.

Articulating ideas between individuals usually helps to provide clarity about issues and often moves people from merely knowing something to understanding it. So this more personal and intimate process can help prepare people for sharing their ideas in the more 'public' forum of the group and, in the process, making for a deeper understanding of their own ideas. Also for the many children who do not have the opportunity to express their ideas and to be listened to by others this process is vital in encouraging their motivation and self esteem. Many of you will know how valuable this has been through the use of Circle Time.

Matthew Lipman in his work with young children over 20 years, shows clearly how this process of dialogue develops thinking skills and general cognitive development. He offers children the opportunity to engage in philosophical debate, getting them to question ideas just as Socrates did in his Greek city state. Ideas such as:

'If I am dreaming am I still alive?'

'If I did not have a brain could I still think?'

'Is it my body which thinks or is it me?'

The aim is to make children think and to challenge some conventional ideas. They are also encouraged to challenge each others' ideas and that of the teacher in a collaborative quest for a deeper understanding of their own ideas and thoughts. An essential part of this process is that they learn to listen to other people's ideas and, very importantly, to be listened to by others. As Lipman says it can be:

> an intoxicating experience for children to have their peers listen to and respect their ideas.

It is clearly a process involving a range of social skills, particularly those of waiting, listening and accepting the ideas of others, even when they disagree with yours.

Lipman used his methods to help 'slow learners' to improve their learning and demonstrates how a group of children who are 12 months behind their peers can make up this 'deficit' in one term.

One important current idea appears to have close links both with learning styles and teaching approaches. This is the idea that individuals might have different 'intelligences'. Gardner (1983) suggests that there could be at least seven realms of knowledge or intelligences: linguistic, mathematical/logical, visual/spatial, musical, interpersonal, intrapersonal, kinaesthetic and that different cultures value these in different ways. David Wood (1998) offers the idea that:

> . . . different societies selectively develop the latent talents of their children in ways that reflect their collective values.

> (Wood, 1998, p. 281)

An important implication for us here is that if we want to develop children's full potential we need to find out what their strengths are and build upon these. We also need to widen our view of what intelligence is. In Western cultures we have valued linguistic and mathematical and logical abilities but other cultures have placed a greater value on kinaesthetic intelligence considering dance and appreciation of graceful movement as important. The importance of interpersonal skills is also of great value in education but in today's schooling environment may not be regarded as highly as the ability to demonstrate competence in literacy or numeracy.

Activity

Recognizing different domains of ability

Do you recognize children with different domains of ability (intelligence?) who have sometimes gone unacknowledged?

Also does the idea of effort and ability have any meaning for you in the way you respond to children's success in school?

One of the ideas I like to emphasize in this whole educational debate is something that might appear rather obvious and that is the distinction between teaching and learning. My years of both teaching and observing others in that activity suggest that we appear to know more about the processes of teaching and focus on it more than we do on what learning is and how it occurs. I feel strongly that today, with the increase in classroom technology, which clearly enhances our teaching methods, there may be a danger of losing sight of what our learners are learning and how they are developing their thinking skills.

What kind of teacher are you?

To conclude this chapter I would like to offer you a framework to informally consider your own values, attitudes and practice. You might wish to engage and debate your thoughts and ideas about a series of questions related to teaching.

This is based on an original questionnaire by McGregor (1982).

Although the questions may appear somewhat stark and a little polarized they can raise some important issues about values and attitudes and approaches to teaching upon which you may wish to reflect and to discuss with colleagues. The range of questions encompasses ideas from previous chapters within this book, but which are vital in a holistic consideration of professionalism and teaching.

I believe that . . .	Agree	Disagree	Comments
Most pupils come to school with some reluctance.			
Most learners can succeed with good teaching.			
My teaching is always rewarding and interesting for all pupils.			
Learners can be divided into two groups: those who 'want to get on' and those who 'want to get away with as little as possible'.			
All pupils can be motivated by effective teaching.			
Every learner works best with plenty of individually-given praise and positive reinforcement.			
Learners are reluctant to learn unless firmly directed.			

I believe that . . .	Agree	Disagree	Comments
Most pupils like an orderly, well-managed work environment.			
More able pupils are difficult to manage.			
It is only natural for pupils to want to do as little as possible.			
Behaviour always has a reason.			
'What's in it for me?' is a reasonable question for learners to pose.			
On the whole, if learners fail to learn it is the fault of the teacher, the school, the curriculum, or poor resourcing.			
Over time, most learners maximize their potential.			
What learners want and what teachers want are different, therefore they will never see eye to eye about work rate and quality.			
Most pupils don't like their work to be appraised.			
Work of a low standard should be stongly criticized.			
Teachers should be prepared to put their foot down if necessary, even at the risk of unpopularity.			
If a pupil who doesn't listen the first time gets additional help, it encourages inattention amongst others.			

I believe that ...	Agree	Disagree	Comments
Staff should go out of their way to behave positively towards pupils who they know do not like work.			
The subject I support and teach demands 'natural flair': either you have it, or you haven't.			
Pupils should be threatened with punishment if they do not work.			
Learners nearly always accept constructive criticism, as they realize that it helps them improve.			
Pupils welcome work if they are given a chance to succeed.			

This form can be photocopied. © *A Toolkit for the Effective Teaching Assistant* 2004.

Questionnaire adapted from McGregor (1982).

Further reading

Donaldson, M. A. (1984) *Children's Minds*. London: Flamingo.

Smith, A. (1998) *Accelerated Learning in Practice*. Network Educational Press.

Sotto, E. (1994) *When Teaching Becomes Learning. A Theory and Practice of Teaching*. London: Cassells.

Using ICT to Support Teaching and Learning

This chapter seeks to provide an introductory overview of what ICT is, and how it can be used to support the teaching assistants' role, within the context of growth and change that technology is bringing to all areas of society. It aims to introduce the reader to some useful resources which will inform and enhance a range of teaching and learning scenarios, with examples of practice being provided by TAs. Whilst the subject matter is large, and the needs of the reader very diverse, it is intended that the contents of the chapter highlight some of the key principles which underpin the use of ICT in the classroom.

It is the application of these principles to their own roles and situations, within the context of rapid growth and change that technology is bringing to all areas of society which is the real challenge facing the educator today.

The chapter aims to allow the reader to explore:

- the growth and impact of the role of ICT in education;

- our own ICT needs as educators;

- what ICT is, and why use it;

- ICT within the context of the whole curriculum;

- developing the use of ICT to support varying levels of learning needs and teaching scenarios;

- planning for effective delivery of ICT;

- using the internet, and obtaining information effectively;

- what the 'digital future' may hold for us.

The key HLTA Standard addressed within this chapter is:

> 2.4   They know how to use ICT to advance pupils' learning, and can use common ICT tools for their own and pupils' benefit.

However, as the Standards are generic by nature, readers will have the opportunity to reflect upon how their own use of ICT may meet a range of Standards.

The growth of ICT in education

The significance with which recent governments have viewed Information and Communications Technology (ICT) skills as being essential in education have reflected a growing commitment to the fundamental belief that:

> . . . the creative and sensitive application of appropriate technology . . . (is concerned with) . . . improving the quality of life of individuals and their range of life opportunities.
>
> (Blamires, 1999, p. 1)

Professor Stephen Molyneux, speaking at the University of Plymouth in November 2003, predicted that in five years time some 50% of workers will be employed in industries that produce or are intensive users of information technology. Charles Clarke, the current minister for education, stated before an invited audience in May 2003 that during a recent survey of all UK job vacancies, some 97% required some element of ICT skills.

The implications of this for the educator are enormous: almost everyone must be equipped to meet the technological demands for the future if they are to be able to work and prosper. Strategies such as those implemented by the National Grid for Learning (NGfL) and New Opportunities Fund (NOF) have ensured that there are policies for meeting targets for delivering internet access to schools and training teachers (but not TAs) in the effective use of ICT. All those working in schools have seen a tremendous change in the profile of ICT, and whilst we can debate the implications of these changes, it is impossible to deny the phenomenal growth of technology – or indeed predict the future directions it might take.

The impact on our own lives is reflected by this small, informal investigation in Cornwall. A group of 20 TAs was asked in March 2003 how many had an email address two years ago. Only two responded positively. Now, all 20 regularly used this technology – an increase of 1,000%.

For an overview of the development of computing and digital technologies, visit the highly informative online Computer History Museum which can be accessed at: www.computerhistory.org

The impact of ICT on the role and responsibilities of the TA

An HLTA Standard relevant to this theme is:

> 3.3.8 They organize and manage safely the learning activities, the physical teachng space and the resources for which they are given responsibility.

On-going research with TAs attending ICT courses strongly suggests that although many TAs cite their roles in using ICT at school as being 'limited', it is apparent that an increasing proportion are becoming involved with 'hands on' use of computers as part of their day, and a small but increasing number are even being given responsibilities for managing computer suites whilst a few others manage their school's websites.

> *The advances in software and hardware technology, the internet, and the ease of their use have had a profound effect on the way teachers view ICT. As confidence and enthusiasm have grown, my job has become vastly more varied.*
>
> (TA (ICT technician), North Devon)

With the rapidly-evolving integration of ICT in all areas of education, it seems highly likely that the future role for many TAs will involve the increased use of ICT, whether this is preparing teaching materials; taking individuals for one-to-one teaching, leading group or whole class sessions; or even managing ICT resources.

In their active participation in supporting the children, teacher, curriculum and school, it is vital that TAs anticipate their future ICT role. This then promotes open, positive dialogue in line with the school development plan and begins to unify the provision and potentially maximize teaching and learning potential for all. Perhaps most importantly, it will empathetically place the educator closer to the cultural contexts within which children are now growing up. In the following practical activity, TAs are encouraged to examine how the growth of technology within school may impact on their roles and responsibilities; it may also be useful to consider any possible changes over a future period, for example, how schools can be proactive in meeting the anticipated needs of potential pupils who might require symbol-supported communication strategies.

> *I may not be working with ICT at present, but perhaps in a year's time I could be working with a pupil who uses an electronic communication aid.*
>
> (TA, Devon)

Activity

Consider and evaluate the changing use of technology in school on your role as a teaching assistant

Assess the use of ICT in your school.

Discuss ICT with your co-ordinator, head of department, or relevant informed member of staff.

Consider how it impacts on your role now, and in the future.

You should examine this within the context of both the school's, pupils' and your own needs, and identify how you might meet the challenges posed, for example, by developing new skills.

The following example illustrates how ICT is impacting on the role of a TA. Consider, using a similar format, the implications of ICT for your school, pupils, TAs in general, and indeed your own role.

School's needs	Possible impact on TA	Impact on me!
Recording and assessment		Need to collaborate – receive information from others; growth of knowledge about individual progression and pupil need
Staff collaboration and communication	Using email, obtaining information from school's intranet	Continuous access to school planning
Creation of presentation materials	Making posters advertising school events	Personal development requirement in conducting web searches
Technical support	Finding out why the printer fails to print	Capacity to manage own time and keep calm under increasing pressure

Pupil's needs	Possible impact on TA	Impact on me!
Creation of resources for pupils to use	Creating starter activities for numeracy and literacy using PowerPoint	Need to find time to transfer resources to PowerPoint, trial presentation, assess outcomes and report back Identify and undertake a course which will help me with the use of PowerPoint
Developing literacy skills	Working with pupil on reading from an electronic 'talking book'	Collaborate with teacher over process and compare records of pupil's previous success in reading with outcomes from 'talking book' sessions

Pupil's needs	Possible impact on TA	Impact on me!

Pupil's needs	Possible impact on TA	Impact on me!

This form can be photocopied. © *A Toolkit for the Effective Teaching Assistant* 2004.

When talking to TAs on the subject of ICT, what always comes across is the wide variation in their practical skills. Many cite a lack of confidence when faced with new ICT learning or challenges. As Waller (Blamires (ed.), 1999, p. ix) notes, whilst educational technology is becoming easier to use, developments still present problems for some users. It is therefore a good idea to establish a baseline of personal ICT skills in order that a pathway of future learning can be identified. Readers should bear in mind that most computer-based activities do not require high levels of skill for their operation; rather, an understanding of a few basic principles and the time to explore and 'play' is the key to the successful use of ICT.

An HLTA Standard relevant to this theme is:

1.6 **They are able to improve their own practice, including through observation, evaluation and discussion with colleagues.**

Activity

The table below is based on an adapted summary of key ICT skills which the Teacher Training Agency (TTA) considers as being essential for trainee teachers to demonstrate competence within. Examine these skills areas and rank your own competency against each, using a scale of 1–5 (1 = unskilled, 5 = very competent).

General skills	Your skill level	Researching and categorizing information	Your skill level
Able to select appropriate software for a task		Sending and receiving emails	
Dragging and dropping objects on the screen		Adding addresses to electronic address book	
Can run more than one application at a time		Carrying out effective internet searches, including refining techniques	
Highlighting text and images		Recognizing characteristics of a web address, e.g. *com, co.uk, edu, ac.uk*	
Navigating around the desktop		Creating bookmarks for visited web-pages	

This form can be photocopied. © *A Toolkit for the Effective Teaching Assistant* 2004.

General skills	Your skill level	Researching and categorizing information	Your skill level
Moving information between software (e.g. by 'copy and pasting')		Downloading files from a website	
Opening items by double-clicking the mouse		Recognizing and using hyperlinks	
Printing (including using the 'print preview' function)		Familiar with the 'browser' buttons and their functions	
Using menus		Can locate files using Windows Explorer function	
Developing and modelling information	**Your skill level**	**Presenting and communicating information**	**Your skill level**
Adding/inserting pictures to a document		Adding a page-break to a document	
File naming and organizing		Adding page numbers	
Inserting columns and rows into a spreadsheet		Changing the format of a document: change font colour, style and size; change background colour	
Adding simple formulae/ functions to cells in a spreadsheet		Justifying the text	
Filing ingoing and outgoing emails		Using word count and spell-check functions	
Adding a record to a database		Replying to emails	
Sorting database columns into ascending/descending order		Adding an email attachment, and opening and saving a received email attachment	

Developing and modelling information	Your skill level	Presenting and communicating information	Your skill level
Querying/filtering information in a database		Carrying out additional email operations: 'copy in' another person, forward to another recipient	
Moving text within a document, e.g. cutting and pasting highlighted text		Inserting hyperlinks into slideshow	
Manipulating digital pictures within a picture editor		Adding transitions and animations to a slideshow	
Finding appropriate images from the internet and placing them into documents by: inserting, copy and pasting		Converting a spreadsheet into a chart	
Changing format of documents into HTML (web-page format)		Adding simple formulae/ functions to cells in a spreadsheet	
Changing format of images in order to reduce memory needed for storage		Labelling a graph	
Placing images into different applications		Downloading images from digital camera and incorporating them into documents and emails	
		Downloading images from scanner and incorporating them into documents and emails	
		Uploading information to a website	

This form can be photocopied. © *A Toolkit for the Effective Teaching Assistant* 2004.

Barriers to the use of ICT exist at all levels, and given the extraordinary growth of ICT this is unsurprising. Computers are highly complex pieces of equipment, and a whole new 'lore and language' has been generated around them. As when visiting any 'foreign territory', it is certainly useful to at least master a few basic words. This language can be overwhelming; Bits, Bytes, ISDN and a plethora of acronyms, abbreviations and new terminology have created a vocabulary with which we are having to become increasingly familiar, and lack of understanding of some of the key nouns and verbs can leave the user feeling rather alienated.

You might wish to investigate two online resources which provide excellent glossaries which can help to explain some of the terminology that you are likely to come across.

- Right Track Learning Center. www.right-track.com/dictionary.htm

- Glossary of Internet Terms. Enzer, M. www.matisse.net/files/glossary.html

Once we have begun to recognize our own difficulties, there comes a need to try find methods of overcoming them. Three key ways of moving forwards are:

(a) to become familiar with the 'geography' of the new territory, and learn about the basic organization of, and terminology associated with, the technology;

(b) to be motivated by the remarkable levels of creativity that ICT can achieve by using a relatively small number of skills;

(c) to explore ICT through play, becoming a confident and competent user of ICT by experimentation and following up any training received by frequent and immediate practice.

It is also important to remember that the computer is after all a machine that can only function when it is *instructed to do so by you*. Where it does gain superiority, however, is in the speed at which it will carry out tasks, and indeed the number of tasks it can carry out simultaneously.

Visualizing how the computer is organized, and indeed functions, can help us to make sense of this highly sophisticated piece of equipment. It is probably best conceptualized as the very piece of equipment it is replacing, namely the office filing cabinet, with each drawer representing a component of the computer's operating system, as illustrated in Figure 6.1. This diagram is also designed to demonstrate the integrated nature of the computer's main functions. For example, music may be downloaded from the internet and saved to almost any area of the computer – from where it can be incorporated into presentations, sent as an email attachment to a friend, or simply played back.

What is ICT?

ICT is not just about using computers; it also embraces, for example, digital photography (still and moving images), audio recording (including CD, DVD, MP3, mini-disk),

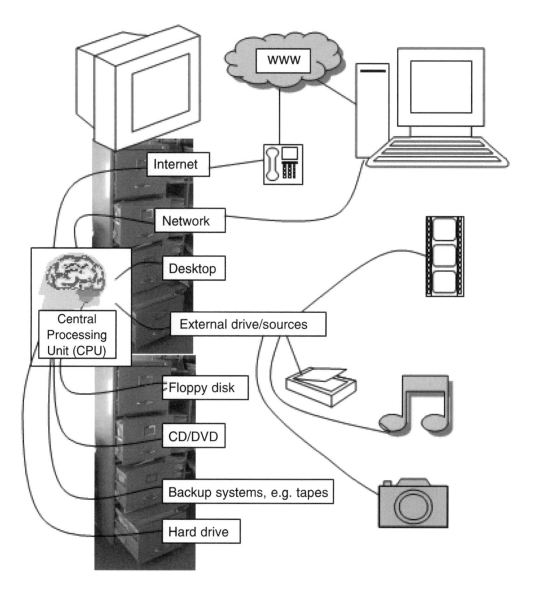

Fig. 6.1 Diagram of the computer as filing cabinet.

multimedia applications, and data collection – all of which are now finding their way into supporting the curriculum, as well as our own lives. After many years of systems being relatively incompatible, the current era of technology development has really focused on making applications at all levels much easier to integrate, and indeed 'user friendly'. The digital medium is not only the 'message' (McCluhan, 1964), but also the universal language of the new technology, facilitating transferability, control and proliferation. It is now a common sight to see tourists using their mobile phones instead of cameras; the phone records the image, from which it can be sent to any email address or compatible mobile phone number.

This potential ease of integration should be seized as a genuine opportunity to enhance teaching and learning and maximize the potential of all pupils. The opportunities to create powerful, multi-media resources can empower and motivate with considerable force.

Why use ICT?

In their report into evaluating the effectiveness of ICT in schools, Ofsted (2002, p. 5) stated that:

> Inspection evidence indicates that ICT is capable of improving the quality of teaching and learning for individuals, even though this is not (yet) the norm in schools. Demonstrating a clear and consistent influence on attainment remains more elusive.

This highly significant report highlighted what many of those in education suspected, namely, that ICT can have a profound impact on the learning for pupils, but that the success of its implementation is dependent on a number of key factors. The British Education and Communications Technology Agency (Becta) identified in a report, 'Primary Schools of the Future – Achieving Today' (2001), five critical factors which *must* be present for good ICT learning:

- good school leadership;
- good general standards of teaching;
- good management of ICT as a subject;
- good classroom teaching of ICT;
- good ICT resources being available.

Becta, in the same report, also identified some compelling evidence of the role ICT played in the raising of levels of pupils' academic achievement. However, the Qualifications and Curriculum Authority (2003) suggests in discussions relating to the teaching of numeracy at Key Stage 3 that we address these questions critically, identifying as to whether the use of ICT is appropriate:

Pedagogical issues:

- Will using ICT help me to teach facts, skills and concepts more effectively?
- Will using ICT help increase pupils' knowledge, give them an opportunity to practise and reinforce some skills, improve their understanding?

Organizational issues:

- Will using ICT help pupils to organize, present and refine their work and communicate their findings?

Ofsted and Becta in the above reports have posed some key questions for schools to answer in order that they can assess their use of ICT:

■ How effectively is ICT being used in subjects across the curriculum in your school?

■ What provision is your school making to ensure that it has access to good quality support services?

■ How well are staff in your school supported in their use of ICT through continuing professional development, ready access to ICT resources and technical support?

■ What strategies does your school employ to ensure that any digital divide is not widened and all young people benefit from the use of educational technology?

■ To what extent is ICT being used to develop higher order thinking and reasoning skills in your school?

■ How does your school measure the impact of ICT on pupils' learning?

Activity

Examine the role that ICT plays in your school, and identify where its use is particularly effective. The following activity draws on the above questions posed by Ofsted and Becta to help you and colleagues begin to evaluate the use of ICT.

Are you aware of the contents of your school's ICT policy?

Have you received training in the use of ICT which is relevant to your work in the classroom?

Are resources well-maintained, with technical support readily available?

Does ICT provide supporting activities for lessons across the curriculum?

Does the use of ICT feature in the planning for the core subject areas?

Is there a strategy for recording the progress that pupils make using ICT?

Activity continued

Is equality of access opportunity by all pupils facilitated, for example, providing relevant software for those pupils with Specific Learning Difficulties?

In what ways is ICT a strength in your school?

In what ways is ICT a weakness in your school?

In what ways does ICT support creativity and higher order thinking in school (cite an example you have seen)?

Consider your findings against the model of 'What makes a good school?' outlined in Chapter 1.

Where to look for curriculum information to support the use of ICT in the classroom

An HLTA Standard relevant to this theme is:

2.2 They are familiar with the school curriculum, the age-related expectations of pupils, the main teaching methods and the testing/examination frameworks in the subjects and age-ranges in which they are involved.

It is true to say that the current drive towards meeting objectives of making administrative communications between education bodies and the government and its agencies 'paper-less' (National Grid for Learning, accessed online: March, 2004) has ensured that all key curriculum documents are located online; in fact, the proportion, if not the overall total, of documents sent to schools in hard (paper) format is falling rapidly. The emphasis now is on the educator to retrieve and review current information from the huge array of government-based web-sites.

The National Curriculum online. This can be viewed at: www.nc.uk.net	The QCA Schemes of Work can be found within the Standards site at: www.standards.dfes.gov.uk
The British Educational Communications and Technology Agency. This is site located at: www.becta.org.uk	The Virtual Teacher Centre. Online resources to support all areas of the curriculum can be viewed at: www.vtc.ngfl.gov.uk
Curriculum Online. One of the latest initiatives aimed at providing resources and information for schools can be viewed at: www.curriculumonline.gov.uk	The National Grid for Learning. This is located at: www.ngfl.gov.uk

Fig. 6.2   Key websites from which curriculum information can be obtained.

Activities

Visit the Virtual Teacher Centre, located at: www.vtc.ngfl.gov.uk and find an online resource to support the QCA Scheme of work for: RE: Unit 6B. Worship and community:

What is the role of the mosque?

You will need first of all to examine the content of the unit, located on the QCA Standards website, and then use the search facility which appears on the Virtual Teacher Centre's homepage.

Identify:

■   the name and address (Unique Resource Locator, or URL) of the web resources;

■   which areas of the unit it clearly addresses;

■   how you might use the resource to support a teaching and learning scenario.

The British Educational and Communications Technology Agency (Becta)

The primary mission of Becta is to disseminate information relating to promoting good and effective practice in the use of ICT, substantiating the assessments made by Ofsted, for example, with both practical and theoretical ways of moving ICT forward in schools. As the government's lead agency for ICT in schools and the learning and skills sector, Becta has a critical role to play in ensuring that ICT is a key element in the four main areas of education. Its extensive website, located at: www.becta.org.uk provides not just practical advice and support for classroom practitioners on using ICT for teaching and learning, but also includes guides to using the latest technologies, the results of research carried out into the use of ICT, and its own online magazine which carries the latest up-to-date news of what is happening in the world of ICT.

Activity

Visit the Becta website (www.becta.org.uk) and locate the Special Educational Needs information sheets which are located in the 'Schools Sector' (ICT in inclusion and SEN).

Think of a pupil you perhaps work with, or you know of in your school, who has a particular difficulty, and find advice on using ICT which relates to his or her need.

Supporting teaching and learning

Using ICT to help meet the needs of pupils with Behavioural, Emotional, and Social Difficulties (BESD)

An HLTA Standard relevant to this theme is:

> **2.9   They know a range of strategies to establish a purposeful learning environment and to promote good behaviour.**

In terms of reaching those pupils who present behavioural challenges in the classroom, there can be no doubt that the use of ICT can have a profound impact on many of these children's desire to learn. As Becta (publication date unknown) points out on its section on ICT and Inclusion,

> For learners with EBD (Emotional and Behavioural Difficulties), information and communications technology (ICT) can provide a non-threatening environment in which to achieve success. For many, learning may have become associated with the fear of failure, both in their own eyes and in the eyes of those around them. The computer can provide a neutral setting in which to experiment, with students confident that they are controlling the

132

pace and level of work. Many learners with Emotional and Behavioural Difficulties (EBD), find it hard to establish relationships, and have little ability or perceived need to relate to others. Using a computer can avoid this problem, and can often offer an entry point for another person to join in alongside, in a non-threatening manner.

Becta points out here that ICT has a certain 'street cred' about it. Many students are stimulated by the fast moving and responsive nature of the technology; its culture and language, as exemplified by the dialect of texting, the seemingly personalized interfaces ICT can offer, and the ease of access to an almost infinite range of dynamically presented information via the web.

ICT has been identified as being an impartial educator. Ulicsak et al. (2001) noted that children see computers as being completely 'non-judgmental'. This research also found that they are certainly more willing to offer responses and share their experiences when confronted by certain types of computer-based tasks, such as when creating a spreadsheet, rather than via an educator – even if they are unsure of their answers. One of the main reasons for this is the ease with which work on screen can be corrected, edited and enhanced compared to paper-based efforts. The computer has the potential to allow pupils of all ability levels to produce a high quality end product, at the pupils' own pace, as well as fostering collaborative learning techniques. Computers, being machines, are also predictable in their responses, offering a level of socially consistent interaction that pupils with BESD may find easier to relate to. Technology has become much more accessible in recent years, with peripherals such as switches, touch-screens and voice activated systems providing interfaces which facilitate inclusion for all. This means that those with physical difficulties, for example, can effectively be offered an opportunity to work from and create stimulating, relevant and motivational resources. However, there needs to be a level of expertise, leadership and determination to unlock such potential.

In Figure 6.3, below, a Year 10 student with challenging BESD, who was also unable to read beyond initial letter sounds of words, created a piece of work independently in which he was able to take and process a digital image of a computer, incorporate it into children's word-processor, and use a 'wordbank' to label the main parts of the PC. He printed his results, and proudly displayed them to his peers. This particular pupil always destroyed any work carried out using more traditional methods, citing them as 'rubbish', and contributing further to his already low sense of self esteem.

Using ICT to support individual learning

An HLTA Standard relevant to this theme is:

3.3.3 They promote and support the inclusion of all pupils in the learning activities in which they are involved.

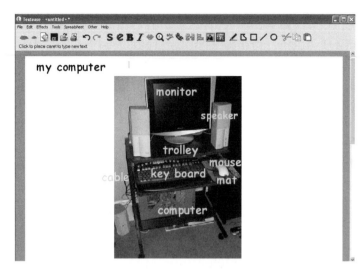

Fig. 6.3 Example of work carried out by a pupil with Behavioural, Emotional and Social Difficulties: a digital photo of a computer was inserted into Softease's 'Talking Textease' programme, with labels being 'dragged and dropped' into position by the pupil.

Textease desktop publishing, word processing, multimedia package, reproduced by kind permission of Softease: www.softease.com

The best computer-based activities in the classroom, as identified by Becta (publication date unknown), enable a wide range of differentiated levels of intervention to be facilitated, by tailoring and adapting tasks to pupils' (individual) abilities and skills.

ICT provides a very powerful instrument for facilitating inclusion of pupils across the curriculum. The best software, combined with these considerations, identified by Becta (2003), should maximize the effective use of technology to support inclusive practices for all through meeting these criteria, namely:

- meeting the range of ability levels: there should be **differentiation** to ensure that tasks are accessible and achievable by students working at all levels;

- objectives and expectations: these should be clear to students and staff;

- the requirements to create **open-ended** tasks to allow student differentiation by avoiding single, predetermined outcomes;

- full student involvement in planning work to maximize ownership of task;

- high quality content which encourages originality and creativity from all students;

- provision of appropriate materials: there should be sufficient, and a variety of, resources to support different student capabilities and learning styles, suitable for the users' ages regardless of ability levels;

- the range of skills students may develop by undertaking any given task;

- the creation of authentic learning tasks which are interesting, motivating and relevant;

- enabling, developing and promoting the independent use of ICT.

Planning for differentiation

The successful use of ICT as a tool for offering differentiated levels of pupil access to the learning is dependent on all staff being aware of the teacher's detailed planning for the class. Familiarity with the use of a relatively small number of good and 'open' resources certainly will also help the educator identify ways of using ICT in learning and teaching scenarios, rather than trying to cope with the application of a huge library of often quite narrowly focused and specialised software.

An HLTA Standard relevant to this theme is:

> 3.3.1   Using clearly structured teaching and learning activities, they interest and motivate pupils, and advance their learning.

Activity

Meeting the pedagogic needs of an individual pupil by establishing a 'profile'

In any individualized learning scenario, it is often helpful to create a profile of a pupil's or group's needs, in order that we can 'visualize' needs more clearly, and create activities and processes that will then help to meet these needs.

By taking a specific lesson or activity, it is possible, by using a template like the one below, to plan precisely how ICT can be used most effectively, in this case to support a KS3 science lesson for a pupil with Down's Syndrome who has reading difficulties. Using a blank copy of this table, identify a specific lesson or learning activity for a pupil, and plan how ICT can be used to support his/her effective inclusion.

Lesson plan for John (When you do this activity – please be very careful to protect the anonymity of all individuals.)

Keystage 3	Subject Science: Unit 7c: Environment and feeding relationships
Pupil's difficulties (brief summary)	John is a Year 7 pupil with Down's Syndrome who attends a mainstream secondary school. He experiences developmental delay in all areas (global), and is operating at achievement levels in literacy and numeracy well below that of his peers. His independent writing skills are limited to writing his name and a few key words, although he can now copy beneath a model. Recently, he has made greater progression with his reading skills, recognizing all the letters of the alphabet, and recognizing by sight approximately 50 key words.
Lesson focus/title	Science: how habitats vary. Pupil has been working on a project which asks him to build up a bank of phrases that will describe various wildlife habitats.
Curriculum objectives for pupil	To use four words, to create descriptive phrases which match photographs.
ICT skills required	To be able to use an on-screen wordbank. To be able to use the mouse buttons and pointer accurately. To print out completed phrases.
Pupil outcomes	To produce a series of four phrases to describe photographs of various habitats. The pupil will first listen to the words being 'spoken' by the computer, before selecting them for his phrase.
ICT support	Four linked *Clicker 4* talking book pages which have been set up to include words relating to the habitats chosen.
Resources	Photographs of four habitats
Other comments	

Lesson Plan for . . . (When you do this activity – please be very careful to protect the anonymity of all individuals.)

Keystage 3	Subject
Pupil's difficulties (brief summary)	
Lesson focus/title	
Curriculum objectives for pupil	
ICT skills required	
Pupil outcomes	
ICT support	
Resources	
Other comments	

This form can be photocopied. © *A Toolkit for the Effective Teaching Assistant* 2004.

Examples of practice

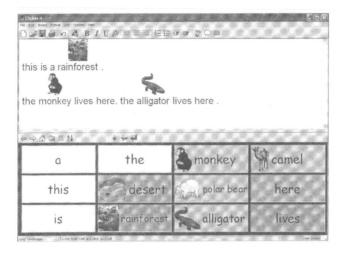

Fig. 6.4 A TA has created an on-screen grid relating to habitats using Clicker 4. By clicking on the cells, graphics, symbols and text can be readily inserted into a document. Particularly useful components are the speech function which will read out the text, and a facility for creating 'talking books'.

Clicker 4 reproduced by kind permission of Crick Software: www.cricksoft.com

Fig. 6.5 Using an alternative method, a TA has created a writing frame which incorporates a 'drop-down' menu facility, allowing the pupil to choose the desired word from a pre-entered list. When the cursor is moved over a highlighted word, the list automatically appears, and when selected, is entered onto the page.

Using ICT to support a pupil with specific learning difficulties

Hardy (2002), along with Sharp et al. (2002), explored five intrinsic properties identified by the DfEE (1998) that ICT offers for pupils, which can be seen as of especial advantage to those who experience learning difficulties:

1   automatic features (allowing storing, transforming and displaying information to be carried out by the technologies);
2   capacity and range (affording access to information locally and globally in different time zones and geographical places);
3   provisional qualities (enabling users to make changes, try out alternatives and keep a 'trace' of the development of ideas, with little risk of loss of content);
4   interactivity (engaging users at a number of levels);
5   social attributes (communication and collaboration).

By considering these attributes within the context of an individual pupil's needs, we can begin to look at very precise ways in using ICT to target specific difficulties – whatever the level or challenge presented.

Activity

Look at the case study below and, in line with the process for creating a pupil-profile illustrated above, identify some key ways that ICT could be used to meet this pupil's needs.

■   Jack is a Year 6 pupil who is high on the Autistic Spectrum Disorder. He requires a very structured learning environment, responding in difficult and indeed challenging ways when faced with something unexpected or inadequately prepared for. His verbal language is predominantly echolalic, and although he can name correctly the activities, events, objects, people etc. who are important to him, he finds great difficulty in organizing basic tasks for himself, such as dressing. He experiences no sensory impairments; indeed, he has a heightened perception of sounds, which can cause him distress at times. His teaching team is focusing on improving his levels of behaviour through developing his understanding of what is going on around him.

Examples of practice

Fig. 6.6 A TA who works with a boy with autism has prepared a slideshow which helps to reinforce the sequence for getting dressed after PE. She has also incorporated a child's voice to make the presentation even more friendly.

Fig. 6.7 A TA has created a set of instructions using Widgit's 'Writing with Symbols 2000' software. This enables a pupil with severe learning difficulties to attach meaning to the written word, and carry out the task with understanding as independently as possible.

Writing with Symbols 2000 (Rebus version) reproduced by kind permission of Widgit Software: www.widgit.com

Considering ICT in relation to learning styles

This section should be read in conjunction with the chapter on Teaching and Learning.

The variety of presentation modes available in the 'multi-media' environment offered by the computer also allows the educator to match an activity to the pupil's preferred learning style(s) – a key factor in ensuring the effective delivery of teaching materials. Because ICT-based information can be presented in so many different ways to a wide audience, the technology can be used to engage almost any conceivable learning scenario, from one-to-one teaching, through to whole classes (and beyond). The increasing availability of data projectors in schools means that software, and indeed 'live' internet-based resources, can be readily used to deliver a numeracy or literacy starter activity, for example, to a class of 30 pupils.

Example of practice

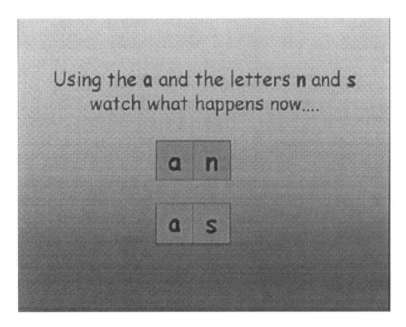

Fig. 6.8 A screenshot from a TA's slide show presentation used to support a literacy starter session focused on developing recognition of vowel sounds. Using animated text-boxes and accompanying sounds, the presentation consisted of vowels which 'flew' into position in order to create short words.

Using ICT to support 'problem-based learning'

An HLTA Standard relevant to this theme is:

3.1.1 They contribute effectively to teachers' planning and preparation of lessons.

A factor that will be seen as being increasingly significant in pedagogical terms is the way that pupils can use the new technologies to support all areas of the curriculum; the dynamics of collaborative and problem-based learning (PBL) scenarios within the classroom situation would be a key way of helping educators to identify how to meet the government's objectives of embedding ICT in all aspects of every day practice (Charles Clarke, 2003).

At its heart, ICT is essentially about investigating and sharing information. Whilst many of us are spending increasing amounts of time in front of the computer screen, we are frequently engaged in tasks that are require collaboration with others – communicating and enhancing our ideas using a global network of knowledge and users – effectively becoming a 'community of learners'. The complexity of modern society almost demands that tasks are too big for one person alone to carry out – they have to be shared and managed amongst groups of like-minded people. The internet is allowing us to do this at a rate which would have been unprecedented even five years ago. In many cases, children have been very quick to recognize this attribute of technology; they will use 'chat rooms' (whether we like it or not), to find out about the latest PlayStation 'cheats', from like-minded, but 'virtual' peers from around the world. In the classroom, problem-based learning simulations and scenarios using computers will offer the chance for pupils to engage in collaborative learning as never before, and educators may well have to redefine in the future the precise nature of what we know as cheating – the ability to collaborate, investigate, evaluate and share information must surely become a higher learning goal, replacing the system of on-going testing of an individual's accumulation of knowledge.

Problem-based learning is, according to Maier and Warren (2000), 'learning by doing. Problems are usually contextualized within (future) workplace settings, roles or creative design. They allow students the freedom to progress through free enquiry and give them the experience of overcoming confusion and frustration (i.e., cognitive conflict that restructures a student's knowledge) prior to finding a solution'.

Good planning is essential if pupils are going to achieve positive outcomes from the collaborative process; individuals should, as far as possible, identify and manage their own learning, whilst maintaining themselves as part of the group.

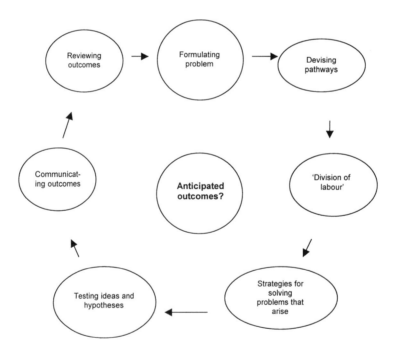

Fig. 6.9   A problem-based learning model for the classroom.

In practical terms, the PBL/collaborative learning model can be readily adapted to the use of ICT in classroom-based contexts, although clearly such learning scenarios must

142

be carefully discussed with colleagues and delivered *as part of a planned programme of study*. In the example below, a pupil who experiences acute literacy difficulties (pupil 1) and a team of three peers in a KS2 classroom are asked to carry out a problem-based learning task, focused on finding out the names of various parts of a plant.

Activity

Using the format below for developing a problem-based learning activity, can you identify and plan an activity for a small group of (three to four) pupils which will encourage them to approach a learning scenario using the collaborative model?

A blank, photocopiable form for completing this activity can be found at the end of the example.

Subject: Science	Outline of PBL scenario:
Focus: Science: **Unit 2B:** Plants and animals in the local environment **Section 4:** Flowering plants	Pupils are asked, in groups of four, to identify seeds from a variety of fruits

What is the problem?	Pupils discuss the nature of the task that has been posed. They look at various ways of reaching an outcome, and decide on the stages they need to go through in order to come up with the results asked for.			
How do we move forward?	The group look at the resources that are available to them: slideshow software, digital camera, microphone, science CD ROM, picture book of plants, website showing plants and their parts. They collect samples and take digital photographs of the various parts which will then be inserted into a slideshow which can be presented to the whole class group.			
	Pupil 1	**Pupil 2**	**Pupil 3**	**Pupil 4**
Assigning roles for our group	To take digital photographs of seeds and fruits	To investigate a science CD ROM about how plants reproduce	To locate a good web-based science/plant resource	To manage the use of slideshow

	Pupil 1	Pupil 2	Pupil 3	Pupil 4
How will we solve the problems that might arise?		To find and use reference materials from CD ROM		To find the class's pictorial guide to using PowerPoint
Testing our ideas – checking that they are right			Check the results against another (web-based) science resource	
Recording and sharing our results	To take digital photos of seeds and insert each image into an individual slide	Adding text to the slide show images		Creating the overall framework for the slideshow, including adding animations, and printing handout materials
Plenary: what did we do well, and what could we improve upon?	Whole class discussion and evaluation of the various outcomes that each group achieved, and what, if the exercise was repeated, would be done differently			

Subject:	Outline of PBL scenario:
Focus:	

What is the problem?				
How do we move forward?				

	Pupil 1	Pupil 2	Pupil 3	Pupil 4
Assigning roles for our group				
How will we solve the problems that might arise?				
Testing our ideas – checking that they are right				
Recording and sharing our results				
Plenary: what did we do well, and what could we improve upon?				

Using ICT to investigate the internet effectively

> The web doubles in size every 90 days . . . Internet use is going up at the rate of 140 persons a second, or 72 million per year.
>
> (Professor Stephen Molyneux, 2003)

An HLTA Standard relevant to this theme is:

2.1   They have sufficient understanding of their specialist area to support pupils' learning, and are able to acquire further knowledge to contribute effectively and with confidence to the classes in which they are involved.

It is, however, in the growth of the internet that we see perhaps the most dramatic development of the use of ICT; it was only in 1989 that the World Wide Web was developed by an Englishman, Tim Berners-Lee, into the format that we know today.

The internet's phenomenal growth is due primarily to its almost completely unregulated nature. Anyone can set up online facilities with relative simplicity, combined with the ease with which anyone with access to a telephone line can download information about any subject.

In the UK, according to the National Statistics Online (2004), the percentage of households that have access to the internet has risen from 9% (2.2 million) in the fourth quarter of 1998, to 49% (12.1 million) in the same quarter of 2003, with 54% of adults using the internet by February 2004. The most common use of the internet amongst the latter group was email (83 per cent). These figures will also, of course, include your pupils, who now have unprecedented access to information and resources to support their study.

It is this size that makes the internet a wondrous, but difficult, and occasionally dangerous place to travel; how do we get exactly the information that we want that is invariably out there somewhere?

Obtaining information effectively from the internet

There are several ways of gaining information from the web. If you have the address, or URL (Unique Resource Locator) of the website, it is usually relatively easy to obtain the information you require. However, many sites are very large, and once having located them there is still a need to navigate their contents. Reading the site index carefully or using a search facility if provided are useful tips to save time and patience.

One of the biggest problems in searching the internet is that there can be far too much information to deal with. Popular search engines, such as Google and Alta Vista, will frequently turn up results to a search running into several thousands of web-pages. However, generally speaking, the information listed beyond the first 20 or so on the list is unlikely (but not always) to be of very specific use. Using additional tools offered by the website (e.g. Google's *image* search tool) will help to refine your investigative criteria, but the key way for searching specific information is to make use of the 'Boolean logic' system which is the key way that search engines such as Google use to identify key elements to search out. There are two methods that are particularly successful for creating 'search strings' that will help the user to find information from a search engine, and these are:

1   Search by the two most important key words and join them with a +, placing the most significant word first, e.g. *ADHD + Diagnosis* in order to find out how ADHD is formally identified. It is certainly possible to insert additional key words using this procedure in order to further refine the search criteria.
2   If you wish to find an exact phrase, e.g. Child Protection Agency (an agency proposed by David Blunkett in January 2003), enclose the *entire* phrase within speech marks e.g. "Child Protection Agency". The search engine will then look for sites where that exact phrase is contained in their metadata.

Some useful search engines:

- Google: www.google.com

- Alta Vista: www.altavista.com

- Yahoo: www.yahoo.com

- Yahooligans (for children): www.yahooligans.com

- Ask Jeeves: www.ask.com

- Webcrawler: www.webcrawler.com

Activity

Find out specific information from the internet, using a search engine, relating to Attention Deficit/Hyperactivity Disorder (ADHD) which identifies or lists:

- diagnostic criteria;

- support for parents;

- tips and advice for implementing strategies in the classroom;

- support for people who themselves have ADHD;

- information relating to recording the effectiveness of strategies used to support the teaching of pupils with ADHD;

- results of recent research into the condition of ADHD.

What makes a good website?

The internet allows web-designers to employ a very wide range of tools which in other media would be almost impossible to integrate. Text, images (still and moving) and sounds can all be used to enhance the appearance of a website; it is obviously going to be an impossible task to design a website that appeals to everyone, but by applying the criteria listed below, we can start to identify the criteria by which we can judge the content, usability and appearance of a web-based resource.

- Ease of use: is the site simple to navigate, and can the required information be found quickly and also able to be relocate on a subsequent visit?

- Quality of information: is it seemingly reliable, thorough and up-to-date? Generally speaking, the more regularly a site is up-dated, the more reliable and relevant the information (but not always).

- Who is the website's creator? *Anyone* can make a web-page, and the majority of websites are in fact anonymous. It is certainly important, especially if the site is a factual one, that it commands a sense of authority.

- Accuracy of information: it is always wise to err on the cautious side when presented with information of any sort in such an open marketplace, and this approach needs to adopted by all users, increasingly so in this media-driven age. When investigating the web, it is useful to know what is the purpose of the information being provided, who it is aimed at, what are the credentials of those who compiled the information, and, most importantly, that what is being presented is the truth. Some facts are easier to check than others, but a clue to establishing whether articles on the web, as with any form of research, are bona fide is whether a good list of resources and references is included. Such references on a website will probably include a list of links to other related sites – always check on these for quality. A key can also be in the web-address suffix; *com* or *co.uk* signifies that the site is likely to have a commercial interest, whilst *ac.uk* denotes that the site is a UK-based academic institution. *Org* and *org.uk* is used by sites that are non-profit making organizations – most charitable organizations will contain this in their address. One of the most valuable ways of developing skills in evaluating websites is to compare two which have similar themes, using a set list of criteria.

- When was it last updated? If a site has been updated recently, that is generally a good sign; in the case of education, things are changing quickly, and it is important to make sure that the information on a site did not pre-date outcomes of recent research or legislation, for example, that a government consultation document, 'live' for a specific period of time, has not been subsequently updated and led to a change of policy thinking.

- Are there a lot of advertisements? Advertisements can be long, rectangular banners at the top, bottom or sides of the screen, or within the page itself. The most irritating type are those that 'pop up' when a site is accessed, and usually indicate that the web host is providing a free service. If a site contains a lot of advertising, we may want to think twice about whether the information on it is unbiased. However, many valuable sites do contain advertising to help support themselves – just look at a page of *The Times* newspaper, for example, and see just how many adverts there are on a page, yet it is still considered to be an authoritative source of information.

■ Appearance: are the pages of the site too 'busy'? Or are they restful on the eyes and designed thoughtfully to present information in an attractive and thoughtful manner?

A note about safe-surfing: it is clearly very easy to retrieve information which is offensive and unsuitable for both children and us – even when accessing the internet from protected networks. Becta has excellent advice on how to address this issue on its website, located at: www.safety.ngfl.gov.uk

Activity

Evaluate and compare objectively two websites which offer information about Down's Syndrome.

Visit the National Down Syndrome Society (US) and the National Down's Syndrome Association (UK) websites, and complete the table below (please note, in the US, Down Syndrome and not Down's Syndrome is the prevailing term for this condition)

Website	National Down Syndrome Society (US) www.ndss.org	The Down's Syndrome Association (UK) www.downs-syndrome.org.uk
Detailed, high quality, factual information listed about the condition?		
Help and support for educators?		
Help and support for parents?		
Help and support for pupils themselves who have Down's Syndrome?		
Ease of navigation (getting around the website, finding out what you want)?		
Presentation (e.g. use of appropriate graphics, are the pages cluttered/distracting advertising)?		
When was the website last updated?		
Are managers of websites contactable?		

This form can be photocopied. © *A Toolkit for the Effective Teaching Assistant* 2004.

Moving forward with ICT: the digital future

With technology that is moving forward at such a pace, it is impossible to make predictions about where ICT will be in five years time, and what its likely impact will be on schools, and indeed us. Hills, cited by Abbott (2001, p. 7) noted, even as far back as 1980, that there would possibly be a '. . . (move) away from the formal educational setting . . . towards a more home-based educational system'. The Teleworkers Association (2003) identified that there were in 2003 a total of 2.113 million people working from home using the 'new technologies', a development that could be replicated in the future by the education sector. Indeed, Illich (1973), as cited by Abbott (2001, p. 116) predicted the inevitable 'disestablishment of schools'.

However, there do seem to be four issues that will almost certainly dominate in the climate of change that is enveloping our society. The increasing spread of broadband connectivity will change the way that we use the internet; high quality video, for example, will be available on demand, software will be remotely provided, being downloaded to any computer in seconds (the BBC already has the go-ahead to dramatically increase its freely available range of educational software).

The second area of change that the technology will facilitate is mobility; the quality and speed of communication between people located in almost any part of the world is not only exceptional, but also, for the first time, reliable and increasingly relatively inexpensive to use. Video-conferencing technology, for example, means that it is now possible for classes to 'virtually' visit experts and centres of interest located literally thousands of miles away.

The third category is one that encompasses all areas, namely the development of online learning communities. Increasingly, groups of individuals with shared interests are forming themselves into groups which will, in all likelihood, never meet face-to-face. Instead, they communicate by text, chat, discussion, audio and video-conferencing in networks spanning the world and which are oblivious to distance and time, and set in an ethos of collaboration and common objectives. Many children already participate in such scenarios, redefining our view of social models and peer-group interaction. Managed Learning/Virtual Learning Environments (MLEs/VLEs), as defined by Whatis.com (accessed online: 6 June, 2004) are now standard in education establishments throughout the world, offering students a huge array of online recources such as curriculum mapping (breaking curriculum into sections that can be assigned and assessed), student tracking, online suport for both teacher and student, electronic communication (email, threaded discussions, chat (web publishing), and internet links to outside curriculum resources.

Lastly, the effects of the socio-economic concept, the 'digital divide', will become an even greater global issue at all levels. Already, great concern is being voiced about the way that many people are being by-passed by the digital revolution; the Third World has very low rates of internet accessibility, and the educational and economic welfare it can bring, meaning that the gap between rich and poor will widen still further. But this divide is affecting sectors of all societies, with access being denied to the web, by various social groups; age, literacy skills, poverty and geographical location are all factors that are contributing to this division. 'Digital democracy' may be high on the government's agenda, but there is still a long way to go before the accessibility now being provided in schools is available to all.

It is the number one myth, as Klieman (2000, p. 8) identifies, that merely putting computers into schools will directly improve learning, and that more computers will result in greater improvements. ICT is a powerful, complex, and flexible tool, but its value depends on human engagement in the learning process which will determine the purposes to be served, and how well the technology is used.

Readers of this chapter, and their schools, will be at varying stages in the acquisition and use of the 'new technologies'; as resources become more universally available, and all access issues are addressed – as they surely will be – the educator will almost certainly be involved in substantial changes in the way they use ICT, not just in school, but in their lives. As Stephen Molyneux stated in his Plymouth conference key-note address (2003), 'the best way to predict the future is to invent it yourself' . . . ICT gives us the power to do this.

Further reading

British Journal of Educational Technology. Oxford: Blackwell.

Gordon, D. (ed.) (2000) *The Digital Classroom – How Technology is Changing the Way We Teach and Learn*. Cambridge, MA: The Harvard Education Letter.

Loveless, A. and Ellis, V. (eds) (2001) *ICT, Pedagogy and the Curriculum*. London: Routledge Falmer.

Appendix: The HLTA Standards

In this book the concentration has been on assessing, developing and honing the skills, knowledge and understanding of individuals employed as teaching assistants and endeavouring to make them more effective in their role through reflection on practice. The current development of Standards for higher level teaching assistants gives an opportunity for all TAs to assess and examine their own strengths and weaknesses against this formal framework.

We suggest that you look at the Standards below and talk about them with colleagues. You might even wish to start looking at your practice and thinking about educational issues in terms of these Standards and collecting evidence of your competence.

Extract from Teacher Training Agency document on the HLTA Standards

Support staff in schools make a strong contribution to pupils' learning and achievement. The National Agreement between government, employers and school workforce unions has created the conditions in which teachers and support staff can work together even more effectively, in professional teams. In this context, some support staff – higher level teaching assistants (HLTAs) – will be able to undertake a more extended role.

The professional Standards set out the expectations of teaching assistants who are identified as able to work at this level.

Teachers' professional training, knowledge and experience prepare them to take overall responsibility for pupils' learning. However, they are not required to take sole responsibility for every aspect of each lesson that is taught. There are times when they will want to draw upon support from a wide range of other colleagues, including HLTAs.

The work of HLTAs complements that of teachers and the roles are not interchangeable.

HLTAs work in a range of different settings and with more autonomy than most other school support staff. Teachers and headteachers, working within the regulatory framework, will be expected to make professional judgments about which teaching and learning activities HLTAs should undertake and what support and guidance they should have.

153

These Standards, and the associated training and assessment, are designed to provide an assurance to teachers, employers and parents about the quality of contribution to pupils' learning that HLTAs can be expected to make.

The Standards apply to HLTAs working in all phases of education and in all areas of school life. They have been designed to be applicable to the diversity of roles in which school support staff work to support pupils' learning. The Standards are also designed to support smooth progression to QTS for those HLTAs with the potential and interest to go on to qualify as teachers.

The Standards for HLTAs

These Standards set out what an individual should know, understand and be able to do to be awarded HLTA status. They are organized in three inter-related sections.

1 Professional values and practice

These Standards set out the attitudes and commitment to be expected from those trained as HLTAs.

1.1 They have high expectations of all pupils; respect their social, cultural, linguistic, religious and ethnic backgrounds; and are committed to raising their educational achievement.

1.2 They build and maintain successful relationships with pupils, treat them consistently, with respect and consideration, and are concerned for their development as learners.

1.3 They demonstrate and promote the positive values, attitudes and behaviour they expect from the pupils with whom they work.

1.4 They work collaboratively with colleagues, and carry out their roles effectively, knowing when to seek help and advice.

1.5 They are able to liaise sensitively and effectively with parents and carers, recognizing their roles in pupils' learning.

1.6 They are able to improve their own practice, including through observation, evaluation and discussion with colleagues.

2 Knowledge and understanding

These Standards require HLTAs to demonstrate they have sufficient knowledge, expertise and awareness of the pupils' curriculum to work effectively with teachers as part of a professional team. They also require HLTAs to demonstrate that they know how to use their skills, expertise and experience to advance pupils' learning.

2.1 They have sufficient understanding of their specialist area to support pupils' learning, and are able to acquire further knowledge to contribute effectively and with confidence to the classes in which they are involved.

2.2 They are familiar with the school curriculum, the age-related expectations of pupils, the main teaching methods and the testing/examination frameworks in the subjects and age ranges in which they are involved.

2.3 They understand the aims, content, teaching strategies and intended outcomes for the lessons in which they are involved, and understand the place of these in the related teaching programme.

2.4 They know how to use ICT to advance pupils' learning, and can use common ICT tools for their own and pupils' benefit.

2.5 They know the key factors that can affect the way pupils learn.

2.6 They have achieved a qualification in English/literacy and mathematics/numeracy, equivalent to at least Level 2 of the National Qualifications Framework.

2.7 They are aware of the statutory frameworks relevant to their role.

2.8 They know the legal definition of Special Educational Needs (SEN), and are familiar with the guidance about meeting SEN given in the SEN Code of Practice.

2.9 They know a range of strategies to establish a purposeful learning environment and to promote good behaviour.

3 Teaching and learning activities

These Standards require all HLTAs to demonstrate that they can work effectively with individual pupils, small groups and whole classes under the direction and supervision of a qualified teacher, and that they can contribute to a range of teaching and learning activities in the areas where they have expertise. They require all

HLTAs to demonstrate skills in planning, monitoring, assessment and class management.

3.1 Planning and expectations

3.1.1 They contribute effectively to teachers' planning and preparation of lessons.

3.1.2 Working within a framework set by the teacher, they plan their role in lessons including how they will provide feedback to pupils and colleagues on pupils' learning and behaviour.

3.1.3   They contribute effectively to the selection and preparation of teaching resources that meet the diversity of pupils' needs and interests.

3.1.4   They are able to contribute to the planning of opportunities for pupils to learn in out-of-school contexts, in accordance with school policies and procedures.

3.2 Monitoring and assessment

3.2.1   They are able to support teachers in evaluating pupils' progress through a range of assessment activities.

3.2.2   They monitor pupils' responses to learning tasks and modify their approach accordingly.

3.2.3   They monitor pupils' participation and progress, providing feedback to teachers, and giving constructive support to pupils as they learn.

3.2.4   They contribute to maintaining and analyzing records of pupils' progress.

3.3 Teaching and learning activities

3.3.1   Using clearly structured teaching and learning activities, they interest and motivate pupils, and advance their learning.

3.3.2   They communicate effectively and sensitively with pupils to support their learning.

3.3.3   They promote and support the inclusion of all pupils in the learning activities in which they are involved.

3.3.4   They use behaviour management strategies, in line with the school's policy and procedures, which contribute to a purposeful learning environment.

3.3.5   They advance pupils' learning in a range of classroom settings, including working with individuals, small groups and whole classes where the assigned teacher is not present.

3.3.6   They are able, where relevant, to guide the work of other adults supporting teaching and learning in the classroom.

3.3.7   They recognize and respond effectively to equal opportunities issues as they arise, including by challenging stereotyped views, and by challenging bullying or harassment, following relevant policies and procedures.

3.3.8   They organize and manage safely the learning activities, the physical teaching space and resources for which they are given responsibility.

References

Abbot, C. (2001) *ICT: Changing Education.* London: Routledge Falmer.

Alliance for Inclusive Education (2000) *The Inclusive Assistant.* London: Alliance for Inclusive Education.

Balshaw, M. (1999) *Help in the Classroom.* London: David Fulton.

Bernet, P. and Savary, L. (1981) *Building Self-Esteem in Children.* New York: Crossroad Publishing.

Blamires, M. (ed.) (1999) *Enabling Technology for Inclusion.* London: Paul Chapman.

Bloom, B.S. (ed.) (1956) *Taxonomy of Educational Objectives: The Classification of Educational Goals: Handbook 1, Cognitive Domain.* New York; Toronto: Longmans.

Bloom, B.S. (1964) *Stability and Change in Human Characteristics.* New York: Wiley.

Bovair, K. and McLaughlin, C. (eds) (1993) 'Counselling in schools': a reader. London: David Fulton.

British Education and Communications Technology Agency (2001) *Primary Schools of the Future – Achieving Today.* www.becta.org/corporate/pressout.cfm?id = 1573.

British Education and Communications Technology Agency *Emotional and Behavioural Difficulties and ICT.* www.ictadvice.org.uk/index.php?sectionm = tl&cat = 002002&rid = 1802&pagenum = l&NextStart = 1 (accessed online: 12 February 2004).

Busher, H. (2001) 'The Micro-politics of change, improvement and effectiveness in schools', in A. Harris and N. Bennett, *School Effectiveness and School Improvement: Alternative Perspectives.* London: Continuum.

Canfield, J. and Wells, H. (1976) *100 Ways to Enhance Self Concept in the Classroom: A Handbook for Teachers and Parents.* Englewood Cliffs, NJ: Prentice Hall.

Centre for Educational Needs, University of Manchester (1999) *The Management and Role of Learning Support Assistants.* London: DfEE.

Coffield, F., Moseley, D., Hall, E. and Ecclestone, K. (2004) *Should We Be Using Learning Styles? What Research Says to Practice.* London: Learning and Skills Research Centre.

Clarke, C. (May 2003) *Using ICT across the Curriculum at KS3.* London: Keynote conference speech.

Department for Education and Employment (1997) *Excellence For All Children: Meeting Special Educational Needs.* London: Stationery Office.

Department for Education and Employment (1998) *Teaching: High Status, High Standards. Requirements for the Courses of Initial Teacher Training.* Circular 4/98. London: DfEE.

Department for Education and Employment (2000) *Working with Teaching Assistants – A Good Practice Guide.* London: DfEE.

Department for Education and Skills (2002) *Consultation on Developing Role of School Support Staff*. London: DfES.

Department for Education and Skills (2003) *Classification of Special Educational Needs*. Consultation document. London. www.dfes.gov.uk/consultations/conResults.cfm?consultationId=1200 (accessed online 4 June 2004).

Donaldson, M.A. (1984) *Children's Minds*. London: Flamingo.

Everard, K. and Morris, G. (1996) *Effective School Management* (3rd ed.). London: Paul Chapman.

Fullan, M. (1982) *The Meaning of Educational Change*. Ontario: OISE Press.

Fullan, M. (1993) *Change Forces: Probing the Depths of Educational Reform*. London: Falmer Press.

Gardner, H. (1993) *Frames of Mind: The Theory of Multiple Intelligence*. New York: Basic Books.

Georgiardes, N.J. and Phillimore, L. (1975) 'The myth of the hero innovator and alternative strategies for organizational change', in C. Kiernan and F.P. Woodford (eds) *Behaviour Modification for the Severely Retarded*. Amsterdam: Associated Scientific.

Gibbs, G. (1992) *Improving the Quality of Student Learning*. Bristol: Technical and Educational Services.

Ginott, H. (1972) *Teacher and Child*. New York: Macmillan.

Goleman, D. (1996) *Emotional Intelligence: Why It Can Matter More Than IQ*. London: Bloomsbury.

Greenhaigh, P. (1994) *Emotional Growth and Learning*. London: Routledge Falmer.

Handy, C. (1994) *The Empty Raincoat*. London: Hutchinson.

Hardy, C. (2000) *Information and Communications Technology for All*. London: David Fulton.

Hay McBer (2000) *Research into Teacher Effectiveness*. London: Department for Education and Employment.

Honey, P. and Mumford, A. (1986) *The Manual of Learning Styles* (2nd ed.) Maidenhead: Honey.

Kleiman, G. (2000) 'Myths and realities about technology in k-12 schools', in Gordon, D.T. *The Digital Classroom: How Technology is Changing the Way We Teach and Learn*. Cambridge, Mass: Harvard Education Letter.

Kolb, D. (1983) *Experiential Learning Experiences as the Source of Learning and Development*. New Jersey: Englewood Cliffs.

Lacey, P. (1998) *Multi-disciplinary Teamwork in Promoting Inclusive Practise* (eds) Tilstone, C., Florian, L., Rose, R. London; New York: Routledge.

Lacey, P. (2001) *Support Partnerships. Collaboration in Action*. London: David Fulton.

Lawrence, D. (1996) *Enhancing Self Esteem in the Classroom*. London: Paul Chapman Publishing.

Lipman, M. (2003) *Thinking in Education* (2nd ed.). New York: Cambridge University Press.

Long, R. and Fogell, J. (1999) 'Self esteem', in *Supporting Pupils with Emotional and Behavioural Difficulties*. London: David Fulton.

Loveless, A. (2002) *Report 4: Literature Review in Creativity, New Technologies and Learning*. Nesta futurelab. www.nestafuturelab.org/research/reviews/cr0l.htm (accessed online 20 March 2004).

McCluhan, M. (1964) *Understanding Media*. New York: Routledge Classics.

McGregor, D. (1982) *The Human Side of Enterprise*. New York: McGraw-Hill.

Maier, P. and Warren, A. (2000) *Integrating Technology in Learning and Teaching*. London: Kogan Page.

Marton, F., Hounsell, D. and Entwhistle, N. (1984) *Experience of Learning*. Edinburgh: Scottish Academic Press.

Maslow, A. (1970) *Motivation and Personality* (2nd ed.) New York: Harper and Row.

Maslow, A. (1999) *Toward a Psychology of Being* (3rd ed.). New York: Wiley.

Molyneux, S. (29 Nov. 2003) *Education in the Knowledge Economy*. Keynote for conference, 'E-learning: strategies for the future'. Plymouth: University of Plymouth.

Murgatroyd, S. and Morgan, C. (1993) *Total Quality Management in Schools*. Bucks: Open University Press.

National Curriculum. www.nc.uk.net (accessed online 10 Jan. 2004).

National Statistics Online: internet access. www.statistics.gov.uk/cci/nugget.asp?id=8.

Office for Standards in Education (Ofsted) (2002) *ICT in Schools: Progress Report April 2002*. London. www.ofsted.gov.uk/publications/index.cfm?fureaction=pubs.displayfile&id=19&type=pdf.

Pedler, M., Burgoyne, J. and Boydell, T. (1986) *A Manager's Guide to Self-development*. London: McGraw-Hill.

Pope, A., McHale, S. and Craighead W. (1988) *Self Esteem Enhancement with Children and Adolescents*. Oxford: Pergamon.

QCA. *Integrating ICT into Mathematics in Key Stage 3: Why Use ICT?* www.standards.dfes.gov.uk/midbins/keystage3/integratingictintomaths.pdf (accessed online 20 March 2004).

Rodd, J. (1994) *Leadership in Early Childhood: The Pathway to Professionalism*. Buckingham: OUP Press.

Rogers, B. (2000) *Behaviour Management: A Whole School Approach*. London: David Fulton.

Sharp, J., Potter, J., Allen, J. and Loveless, A. (2002) *Achieving QTS, Primary ICT – Knowledge, Understanding and Practice*. Exeter: Learning Matters.

Sharp, P. (2001) *Nurturing Emotional Literacy*. London: David Fulton.

Smith, A. (1998) *Accelerated Learning in Practice*. Stafford: Network Educational Press.

Sotto, E. (1994) *When Teaching Becomes Learning. A Theory and Practice of Teaching*. London: Cassells.

Teacher Training Agency. *ICT Skills Test Content*. www.tta.gov.uk/php/read.php?sectionid=115&articleid=376 (accessed online: 28 March 2004).

Teleworkers Association. www.tca.org.uk (accessed online).

Tilstone, C., Lacey, P., Porter, J. and Robinson, C. (2000) *Pupils with Learning Difficulties in Mainstream School*. London: David Fulton.

Tuckman, B. (1965) 'Developmental sequence in the development of small groups'. *Psychological Bulletin*, Vol. 63.

Ulicsak, M. et al (2001) *Raising Awareness in Children of Group Skills Using an Expert System*. San Antonio: AIED conference proceedings.

Visser, J. (1993) *Differentiation Making it Work*. Stafford: Nasen Enterprises.

Whatis.com whatis.techtarget.com/definitin/0.,sid9 gci866691,00.html (accessed online 6 June 2004).

Whitaker, P. (1998) *Managing Schools*. Oxford: Butterworth.

White, M. (1995) *Raising self-esteem: 50 activities*. Cambridge: Daniels.

Wood, D. (1998) *How Children Think and Learn: The Social Context of Cognitive Development* (2nd ed.). Oxford: Blackwell.

Woolhouse, M. and Jones, T. (2001) *Teaching the Post – 16 Learner: A Guide to Planning, Delivering and Assessing Learning*. Plymouth: Northcote House.

Vygotsky, L. (1962) *Thought and Language*. Cambridge, Mass.: MIT Press.

Index

Added to the page number 'f' denotes a figure.